Mend It, Wear It, Love It!

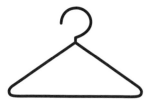

Mend It, Wear It, Love It!

STITCH YOUR WAY TO A SUSTAINABLE WARDROBE

ZOE EDWARDS

Contents

Introduction

Today's rapid cycle of production, buying, and disposal of clothing impairs our ability to feel satisfied and connected with our wardrobes. It's time for a new, slower approach to repairing clothes and to cherishing what we have.

The fundamental source of happiness is relationships. So, it's time to build a healthier relationship with our wardrobes. Let's push back against the concept that pleasure can only be found in the next new thing.

This book gives you the skills to create and update your own sustainable wardrobe of outfits based on what you already own.

Clothes shopping habits

Over the past decades, the speed at which we collectively buy, use, and discard clothing has accelerated dramatically. Research by Greenpeace shows that we consume 60 percent more clothing than we did even 15 years ago. According to the American Apparel and Footwear Association (AAFA), at the beginning of the '90s, Americans bought 40 new garments a year on average; by the end of the decade, it had risen to 65 garments per year.

What's in your wardrobe?

It's time to analyze the clothing you already have. You may be surprised. The average American woman has $550 of unworn clothing in her closet—a massive waste of money. And what we do wear, we use only about seven times before we throw it away. We have entered a state of permanent dissatisfaction with the clothing that we own, and we've been encouraged to believe the only way to move forward is to have a clear out and buy yet more clothes.

Bucking the trend

Well, how about you seek satisfaction and joy in the things you already have, instead? Come on a journey to rediscover and

According to the AAFA, shoppers bought 60 percent more clothing at the end of the 1990s than they did 10 years previously.

When you take the time and effort to repair or improve a garment, you will value it and, more importantly, enjoy wearing it.

reconnect with your existing wardrobe. It's hard to build relationships with items that are as ever-changing as the contents of your fridge. So, establish a status quo and resist the urge to buy anything new for now. You'll need time and brain space to move toward a more fulfilling connection with your clothes.

What needs mending or fixing?

First, you need to identify which items you're just not wearing any more. With these garments separated out, it's time to figure out what the problems are so you can address them. For some, the issues will be obvious: the hem is hanging down in one place or a strategic button popped off, for example. With others, the problems will be harder to identify; they always felt "meh."

If the reason you're not wearing a particular garment isn't glaringly obvious, perhaps you need a prompt. Leaf through the inspirational ideas within this book to see if switching up the buttons is what's needed, or if adding new pockets or removing sleeves is the way to go. Whatever you decide, this book gives you the practical know-how to rework those items and bring them back into regular wardrobe rotation.

Sewing novices welcome

Panic not: no prior knowledge or experience of sewing is required. This book starts at the very beginning, by providing a guide to the essential equipment you need. With clear explanations and illustrations, it will lead you through each step to fix common clothing malfunctions, as well as to apply clever alteration techniques. You don't need a sewing machine, but if you have access to one there are helpful tips to get you started and suitable alternatives where possible.

Satisfaction, guaranteed

Once you've mended your first item, you can go on to bring new life to other unloved garments. When you take the small amount of time and effort to repair or improve a garment, you will value it and, more importantly, enjoy wearing it. The benefits of learning and developing new skills—and taking the time to focus on completing a task using your hands—will be fully felt.

Learning new skills doesn't stop with mending and customizing clothes. Be sure to read the all-important sections on caring for and storing your clothes.

So, what are you waiting for? Just remember to take it slow!

The lowdown on "fast fashion"

Fast fashion has huge human and environmental costs, and as a society we should be consuming far less of it. So, let's have a closer look at the impact of those irresistibly cheap T-shirts.

But what is fast fashion exactly? Well, it's all that inexpensive clothing, produced rapidly by mass-market retailers, in response to the latest trends. It's cool, it's cute, it's cheap, and there'll be something different on the racks the next time you enter the store, as clothing manufacturers race to reproduce the latest catwalk and celebrity looks. But the speed of this is the very definition of unsustainable. The truth is no clothing should be that cheap.

Who picks up the bill?

So, if the consumer isn't paying its true cost, where is the shortfall being made up? Partly, it's in the low quality of the fabrics used and the finishing and manufacturing processes. And, more tragically, the cost of production is kept low by paying fabric and garment workers very little and offering poor working conditions. When the ills of fast fashion are being documented, it's usually an image of an exhausted garment worker hunched over a sewing machine that comes to mind, so let's start there.

The human costs

On April 24, 2013, in Bangladesh, an eight-story concrete building called Rana Plaza collapsed. The building contained many factories used by fast-fashion brands. Caused by negligent construction, the

Only 2 percent of the 40 million garment workers around the world earn a living wage—it effectively amounts to modern-day slavery.

collapse took the lives of 1,134 garment workers and injured another 2,500. Poor conditions and scant safety measures are common in factories producing fast-fashion clothing, and sadly the Rana Plaza tragedy is far from the only deadly incident.

Garment workers are disregarded and undervalued, with only 2 percent of the estimated 40 million garment workers around the world earning a living wage—it effectively amounts to modern-day slavery. Attempts to unionize and to campaign for improvements in safety, conditions, wages, sick pay, and job security are kept in check by the threat of job losses and even documented acts of violence.

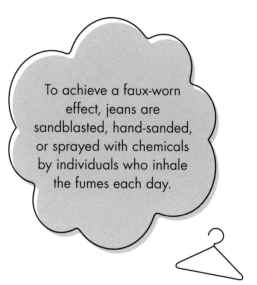

To achieve a faux-worn effect, jeans are sandblasted, hand-sanded, or sprayed with chemicals by individuals who inhale the fumes each day.

The system is unsustainable

But the problems faced by garment workers are not simply caused by factory owners and their need for profit. Workers and their families are trapped in poverty, because a rise in workers' pay results in higher costs for the factory, which in turn would likely mean the factory losing a contract to another that has offered a lower bid to the fashion brand's tender.

The issues are systemic: responsibility must travel up the chain to be shouldered both by the brands themselves for their commitment to keeping the cost of their products so low and by the consumers who have got used to paying so little.

It's almost impossible to list every job involved to produce every piece of fast fashion, but it's likely that almost all of these jobs are poorly paid in unhealthy working conditions. Every sparkly top has had its beads and sequins laboriously stitched on by hand, often by the small fingers of children. Every pair of faux-worn jeans has been sandblasted, hand-sanded, or sprayed with chemicals to achieve the effect by (often poorly protected) individuals who inhale the fumes each day.

Global issue with local problems

The environmental costs, which we'll come to, also have an effect on the local populations indirectly involved in the garment industry. From regions facing drought due to water supplies being diverted to grow cotton in India and the Middle East, to local pollution around fabric-processing plants due to the leaching of toxic chemicals and dyes into waterways.

Charities around the world, such as Fair Trade Federation, Fashion Revolution, and TRAID, campaign to support and advocate for garment workers, and work to hold brands and governments to account to protect their human rights. Supporting these charities is an excellent way to make a difference straight away.

How fashion affects the planet

But it's not just humans affecting and exploiting other humans in the pursuit of trend-led, affordable attire. Studies have revealed that the clothing industry is the second-most polluting industry on Earth.

Fabric and clothing production processes emit greenhouse gases—the biggest contributor to today's most pressing issue: climate change. Globally, the fashion industry produces 3.6 billion tons (3.3 billion metric tons) of CO_2 per year—almost matching the carbon footprint of the entire European Union.

Synthetic or natural?

In addition, many fibers in clothing are sourced from fossil fuels as well. Synthetic fibers (for instance, acrylic, polyester, elastane, Lycra, Spandex, and nylon) are plastics, formed from polymers obtained from petroleum and other by-products of fossil fuels. When these synthetic fabrics go through a washing machine, they release tiny plastic fibers (microplastics) into the waterways. Marine life consumes these microplastics, which enter the food chain.

Speaking of water, cotton, often lauded as one of the most sustainable of fibers, is responsible for a staggering amount of global water consumption. Recent research has shown that it takes 2,000–2,640 gallons (7,570–10,000 liters) of water to make a single pair of jeans.

Precious water resources

The extraction and diversion of water to use in cotton growing is a massive problem in many countries, predominantly in Asia. With a population of 1.38 billion people, access to safe water is a major issue for some in India. Nevertheless, India's cotton industry consumes the same volume of water in a year that could supply 85 percent of its inhabitants with 26 gallons (100 liters) of water every day.

The use of water for growing crops, particularly cotton, has resulted in the

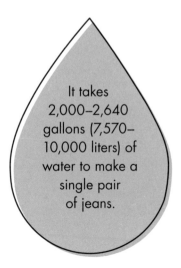

It takes 2,000–2,640 gallons (7,570–10,000 liters) of water to make a single pair of jeans.

desertification of some areas, such as the Aral Sea on the borders of Kazakhstan and Uzbekistan. The speed of its disappearance is shocking: in 1960, the Aral Sea was the biggest inland sea in the world. The fisheries and communities that relied on it have been decimated, and what remains is increasingly polluted by fertilizers and pesticides.

How textiles are made

Sadly, pesticides, herbicides, and fertilizers impact the local population wherever non-organic natural fibers are grown for clothing production. It is impossible to prevent them from reaching neighboring farms, nor to stop the run-off into local waterways.

The processing of many types of fiber destined to become fabric also requires vast quantities of harmful chemicals. Regenerated fibers including rayon/viscose, for instance, started life as wood pulp. These tough plant materials are broken down using a chemical and mechanical process involving sodium hydroxide, carbon disulfide, ammonia, and other chemicals depending on the fiber source. This forms a viscous liquid that is then spun into threads using sulfuric acid. As well as the environmental hazards, exposure to some of these chemicals has been proven to lead to a host of detrimental effects on the health of textile workers, including nerve damage, heart disease, mental deterioration, and strokes.

The production of regenerated fibers has caused deforestation of rainforests, resulting in the displacement of communities and habitat destruction for many species, and ancient forests are being cleared for lucrative bamboo plantations for bamboo textiles.

All such a waste

At the other end of the life of a garment, the US alone is responsible for sending 21 billion pounds (9.5 billion kg) of clothing to the landfill every year. Synthetic fibers, which are effectively plastic, are unable to biodegrade. And even though fabrics made from natural fibers (cotton, wool, linen, hemp, and silk) and regenerated fibers (rayon/viscose, bamboo, Tencel/lyocell, modal, cupro) are able to biodegrade, they will release toxic chemicals into the ground from the finishes and dyes they carry.

Then, there is the CO_2 produced from the transportation of fibers, fabrics, and finished garments around the world. A single garment will likely have clocked up thousands of miles (kilometers) of travel before arriving at the store, ready for you to buy it and take it home.

The future of slow fashion

We need to play our part by embracing the concept of slow fashion. Being able to prolong the life of the clothes we own and wear already is the first step. We can't undo the impact of the clothes we have already bought, but we can take meaningful steps going forward to mend, wear, and love those clothes more.

The Basics

Your basic sewing kit

You may be lucky and own some of these items already. If not, basic sewing kits are available that already include most of the items covered here. Over the next few pages, we list everything you need for repairing clothes by hand.

Once upon a time, it was common for every household to own a basic (or not so basic) sewing kit. Perhaps you have some memories of a sewing kit that used to belong to older family members. Well, it's time you got your very own! Think of it as a rite of passage for any adult committed to caring for their clothes. Then, hopefully, as you repair and rework one garment after another, over time you will create memories with your own trusty little kit. Like how you rescued the hem of your favorite work trousers. Or the time you repaired the topstitching on your most flattering jeans. Or that other time when you saved your dignity by replacing the most "strategic" of buttons on your blouse!

Ah, happy memories.

Tape measures

Fancier, retractable tape measures are available, but the basic ribbon kind works perfectly fine!

Fabric-marking tools

A wide range of fabric-marking tools are available, from the basic triangle-shaped tailor's chalks and chalk wheels that dispense chalk dust, to marker pens with ink that disappears when you iron or wash it. Buy whichever tool appeals to you and experiment with using it.

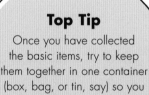

Top Tip

Once you have collected the basic items, try to keep them together in one container (box, bag, or tin, say) so you can grab them quickly when a repair or alteration becomes necessary.

TOOLS FOR MARKING AND MEASURING

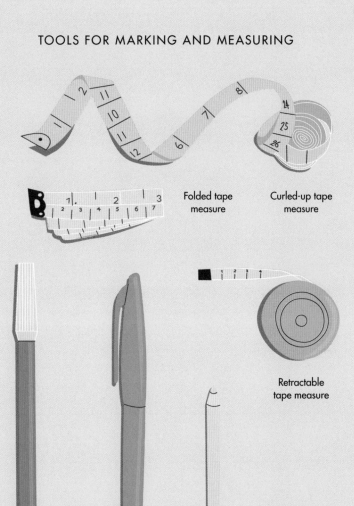

Folded tape
measure

Curled-up tape
measure

Retractable
tape measure

Water-erasable
marker pen

Heat-erasable
marker pen

Chalk pencil
with brush

Tailor's
chalk

TOOLS FOR SEWING, PINNING, AND SNIPPING

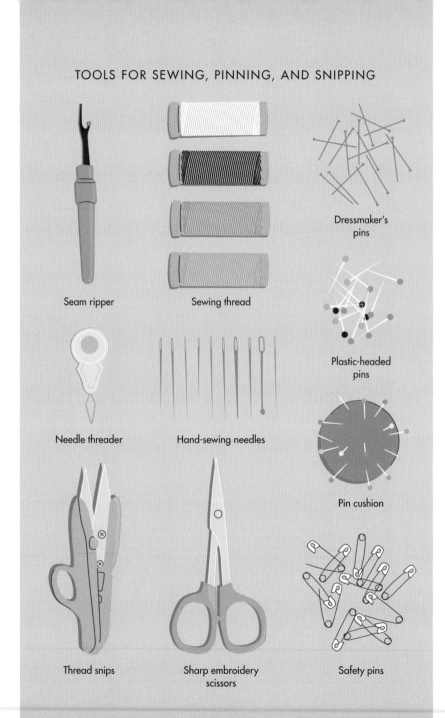

Seam ripper

Sewing thread

Dressmaker's pins

Needle threader

Hand-sewing needles

Plastic-headed pins

Pin cushion

Thread snips

Sharp embroidery scissors

Safety pins

Seam ripper

Also known as a stitch ripper or quick unpicker, this sharp metal hook with a plastic or wooden handle (and safety cover) is useful for the careful removal of stitches. Using scissors or snips to remove stitches is more likely to result in holes in the fabric.

Sewing thread

Go for spools of polyester or 100 percent cotton thread made by a known brand, such as Gütermann or Coats & Clark. Cheap or very old sewing threads are liable to break. If you bought a sewing kit that includes thread, treat yourself to some stronger, higher-quality stuff anyway. It's a good idea to keep a small color range in your kit (black, white, navy, red, gray, and cream) that should cover most of your projects, and add other colors to your collection as you need them.

Needle threader

This simple metal device helps you thread through the eye of a needle without the aid of a magnifying glass. It can be invaluable when using embroidery floss or other multistranded thread.

Hand-sewing needles

Try to find a mixed pack that includes needles in a range of thicknesses, which will be suitable for different thicknesses of fabric.

Pins

A container of sharp pins can help you keep things in place during a repair—only an octopus could successfully complete every project without some pins! The little plastic shapes or spheres on the ends of pins make them easier to pick up, though these will melt if touched by a hot iron. A pin cushion is handy to store pins while you're working.

Safety pins

A few safety pins in a range of sizes will come in very handy. They can be used instead of pins for some projects to keep things in place, and you will be less likely to prick yourself while using them. Safety pins are also invaluable for threading elastic through a channel when making an elasticized waistband or cuff.

Small, sharp scissors or thread snips

A basic, store-bought sewing kit may not include scissors but they are a necessary item. Cheap thread snips are available in most craft stores, but even sharp nail scissors will do—you just need something small with a sharp point to make precise cuts.

Other equipment and useful supplies

For tackling more involved repairs or alterations, and for creating a more professional finish, you will need to invest in a few extra items. Many repairs will also require what are known as "notions"—ribbons, trimmings, buttons, and fasteners, which can be found at most craft stores.

This is next-level business: when your sewing kit grows and can no longer be kept all together in a cookie tin! Some additional pieces of equipment will allow you to create a flawless finish for your repairs and alterations and will broaden your options of the types of projects you will be able to undertake. What additions you end up collecting from the following list will depend on your personal style and creative vision.

Fabric scissors

You'll need a pair of large, sharp scissors for repairs and alterations that involve cutting fabric, such as shortening hems and adding patches. Pinking shears help reduce fraying by cutting a zigzag edge. Keep fabric scissors for fabric. Using them for other tasks, such as cutting paper, will blunt them, and blunt scissors will not only cause frustration but may also damage the fabric or garment.

Iron

Most households have an iron, and it will allow you to improve the finished look of your repair or alteration. It is essential for applying patches and pockets, and using iron-on interfacing. Make sure the bottom is clean and free from any burned-on residue.

Sewing machine

A machine will make most repairs and alterations quicker and more professional-looking. For advice on using a sewing machine, see pp.26–29.

Ironing board

Obviously an ironing board goes hand-in-hand with an iron, but can also provide a useful surface for resting your project on while you work. A heat-resistant surface, such as a kitchen countertop, covered with a clean towel could be a substitute in a pinch.

TOOLS FOR NEATER FINISHING OF FABRIC

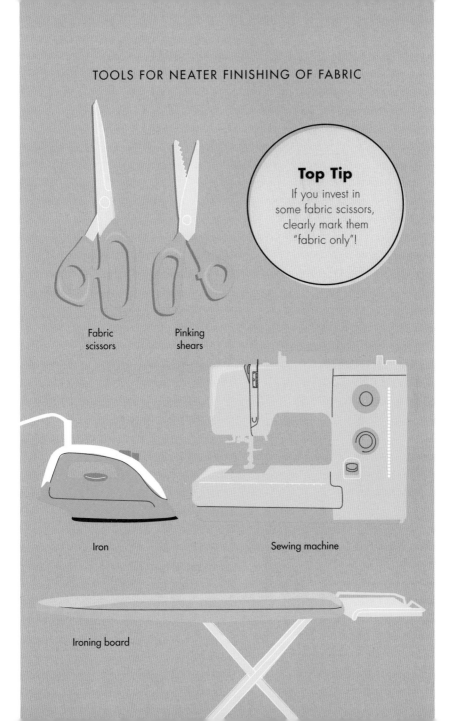

Top Tip

If you invest in some fabric scissors, clearly mark them "fabric only"!

Fabric scissors

Pinking shears

Iron

Sewing machine

Ironing board

HANDY-TO-HAVE ITEMS AND NOTIONS

Fabric scraps

Top Tip

Iron-on patches often start to peel off after a wash or two, so it is a good idea to stitch around the edges after the initial application.

Buttons

Iron-on interfacing

Elastic

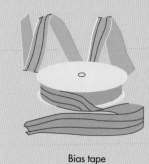

Bias tape

Darning mushroom

Darning yarn

Fabric scraps

Create patches, pockets, additional lengths for hems, and reinforcement for worn-through areas with small pieces of fabric. Harvest fabric scraps from old items that are beyond repair. Particularly useful scraps include denim, T-shirt jersey, and woven cotton (think old shirts).

Buttons

You may need to replace one rogue button that went MIA, or you might wish to swap all the buttons on a garment to transform its look. Like fabric scraps, buttons can be removed from old clothes. Always keep the spare buttons that come attached to your store-bought clothing in a safe place.

Bias tape

Sold in packs or by the yard (meter), bias tape is a long, narrow, continuous strip of fabric with its edges folded toward the center. It is applied over a raw or worn edge to create a new, stronger finish. It's available in a wide variety of widths and colors so, like elastic, you might want to buy this on a project-by-project basis.

Iron-on patches

If you like the look of ready-made, iron-on patches, then they are a great tool for quickly covering up a hole or stain. If you see any that appeal to you, buy them to have on hand.

Iron-on interfacing

Also known as fusible interfacing, this fabric-like material is available in white or charcoal and in a variety of thicknesses. Interfacing is used to stabilize or add additional structure to an area of a garment. Match the thickness of interfacing to the weight of your fabric; for instance, use a lightweight interfacing on fine fabrics and a heavyweight version for thicker fabrics such as denim. One side of iron-on interfacing has tiny, dry spots of glue that are activated by the heat of an iron; always use a pressing cloth (see p.49) or the glue will end up on your iron or ironing board!

Elastic

This stretchy material is available in a variety of types, widths, and colors. Buy elastic on a project-by-project basis to start with. But if you buy slightly too much each time, you'll end up with a stash for future projects that will save you a trip to the store.

Darning mushroom

Darning is made easier using a wooden tool called a "mushroom" (or "egg"). It provides a smooth, curved, hard surface that you hold behind the damaged area. If you don't have one, you could try using an orange or the base of a drinking glass.

Darning yarn

Packs of darning yarn are cheap and available in lots of colors—choose yours to make your repair blend in or stand out.

Mend Your Clothes

Introduction

Our clothes work hard for us. They keep us warm and comfy, look great, and say a lot about who we are. So, when they start to show signs of all this work, don't we owe it to them to pick up that needle and thread?

Before we get into the techniques to deploy against the signs of wear and tear, first let's consider our mind-set. At this point, you may be feeling a bit nervous about wielding pins and needles (let alone scissors!) anywhere near your well-loved garment, and wondering whether it's such a good idea after all. Please internalize the sentiment that any repair that extends the life of a garment by even one more wear is a major success and should be celebrated. By even attempting to make your clothes last longer, you are an active participant in the slow-fashion movement—congratulations!

Bold or subtle?

A garment repair can sit anywhere on the spectrum from "super-neat and invisible to the naked eye," to "a glaringly obvious extension of the life of the garment." Explore #visiblemending online to investigate and revel in the rationale of this approach. It is shared by many who like to highlight, not hide, the journey their clothes have been on.

The role that a garment plays in your wardrobe and your personal style will affect which approach you choose for a specific repair. Whatever you are aiming for, please don't think that a mend needs to

Any repair that extends the life of a garment by even one more wear is a major success.

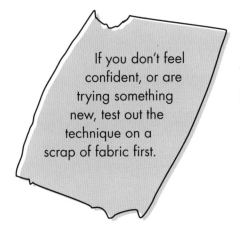

If you don't feel confident, or are trying something new, test out the technique on a scrap of fabric first.

look perfect, or even vaguely neat, to be a success; but it's a good idea to follow some basic rules (see right) for the best results.

Flex newfound skills

The techniques included in this book offer a great foundation for you to tackle most garment repairs. Over time, as issues with your clothes arise, you will get the chance to test out and become familiar with these techniques. It is likely that you'll have great success with some, yet others might take a few tries to achieve the effect that you were hoping for.

Each repair technique in this book is suitable for a beginner. Yet, in reality, there may be a number of different ways to approach any repair job. Feel free to experiment and adapt these techniques if you wish, apply them in a different way, or even develop some of your own.

Have fun, get crafty, and be proud!

To increase the chances of successful repairs, follow these basic rules:

- Once you notice a repair is called for, do not wear the garment again until you have dealt with the problem. Don't wash it either. Continuing to wear or washing the garment before you mend it will very likely make the issue worse and will therefore be more difficult to repair later on.
- Don't attempt to repair a garment while wearing it. You need to lay the garment out and properly inspect the issue to be able to make the best repair possible.
- Try to repair your garment in good lighting. Dark-colored garments are particularly difficult to work on in poor or artificial light.
- If you don't feel confident, or are trying something new, test out the technique on a scrap of fabric first. It's OK to take your time—this is slow fashion after all.
- If the fabric is delicate, fine, fraying rapidly, or super-expensive, consider taking it to a tailor or alterations expert. It's OK to pick your projects. When you collect the repaired garment, ask them how they approached the repair, so perhaps you can try something similar another time.

Using a sewing machine

To make your repairs speedier and give them a neater finish, use a sewing machine. Banish any bad memories from school home ec lessons (if you even had any), and if you can beg, borrow, or steal a machine, why not give it a try?

There are a number of basic functions that you will need to get the hang of initially—winding a bobbin, threading the machine, selecting and adjusting the stitch, and positioning your project ready to be sewn. Assuming you are not the machine's owner, and they are unable to give you a lesson, find out if the machine's manual can walk you through these steps. If you cannot get your hands on a physical version, you may be able to buy a PDF copy or locate a video tutorial; search online for the brand name and model number of the machine.

Once you've learned the machine's basic functions, discover these handy tips to help you toward sewing success.

Tip 1: Use a super-sharp needle

Buy a new pack of sewing machine needles that include a range of sizes (usually from 8 to 16). Most machines will take universal needles, but some (usually older) models use a different type. Do match the needle to the type of fabric, too: universal needles are suitable for woven fabrics but jersey and stretchy fabrics call for a ballpoint needle.

Change the needle of your sewing machine regularly as it's hard to see if it has been damaged. Sewing with a damaged or blunt needle can, in turn, damage the fabric of the item you are trying to repair.

Tip 2: Use the right size of needle

Always match the size of needle to the thickness of the fabric you are about to sew (see table, below). Basically, the larger the number, the larger the needle.

Needle size	Type of fabric
8(60) and 10(70)	lightweight fabrics, such as cotton lawn, silk, and voile
12(80)	medium-weight fabrics, such as jersey, poplin, shirting, and linen
14(90) and 16(100)	heavyweight fabrics, such as cotton drill, denim, and corduroy

THREAD A SEWING MACHINE IN SIX EASY STEPS

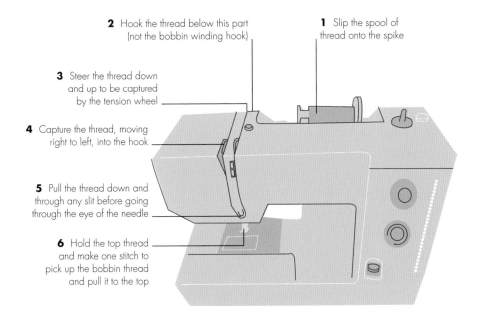

2 Hook the thread below this part (not the bobbin winding hook)

1 Slip the spool of thread onto the spike

3 Steer the thread down and up to be captured by the tension wheel

4 Capture the thread, moving right to left, into the hook

5 Pull the thread down and through any slit before going through the eye of the needle

6 Hold the top thread and make one stitch to pick up the bobbin thread and pull it to the top

A MIXED PACK OF NEEDLES

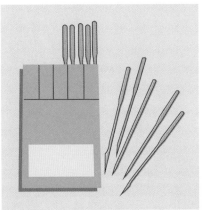

INSERT THE NEEDLE CORRECTLY

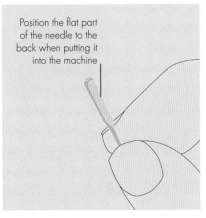

Position the flat part of the needle to the back when putting it into the machine

IS THE TENSION RIGHT?

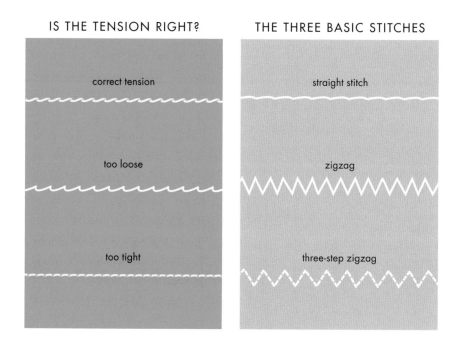

correct tension

too loose

too tight

THE THREE BASIC STITCHES

straight stitch

zigzag

three-step zigzag

FAMILIARIZE YOURSELF WITH THE MACHINE

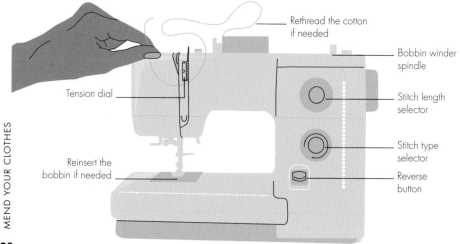

Rethread the cotton
if needed

Bobbin winder
spindle

Tension dial

Stitch length
selector

Stitch type
selector

Reinsert the
bobbin if needed

Reverse
button

Tip 3: Get to know the machine

Refer to the manual/tutorials to get the machine ready: wind and insert a bobbin, insert a new needle, and thread the machine. Also, check the tension dial is set as stated in the manual. Then, run a test on a fabric scrap. If possible, practice on a fabric that's similar in type and thickness to the garment you are about to mend.

Select a straight stitch and sew a few rows, then take the fabric off the machine and have a look. Check to see if the stitch looks even on both sides of the fabric. If there is a mess of loops or the stitches on one side look much looser or tighter than on the other side, carefully rethread the machine and reinsert the bobbin. It could be that you missed a key threading point.

Tip 4: Give the machine some TLC

If you have followed the manual and/or relevant tutorials, and the other tips listed here, but the machine refuses to function properly, it may well be time to bring in a professional. Sewing machines, particularly older ones, require occasional maintenance to stay in good working order. And even newer models that have been left unused or have suffered a mishap might need some TLC from a servicing and repairs person.

Tip 5: Learn the basic stitches

When the machine is stitching nicely, you can then select the most suitable stitch for your repair. Recommended stitch types are specified on each repair technique page, but the most useful stitches to have in your arsenal are straight stitch, zigzag stitch, and three-step zigzag stitch. All but the most basic of sewing machine models should allow you to adjust the length and width of the different stitches, should you need to. Always test your selected stitch and any adjustments you make on a scrap of fabric before starting your repair.

Tip 6: Find the reverse function

Always use the reverse stitch (backstitch) at the beginning and end of every row you sew to secure the thread, otherwise your repair is likely to come undone.

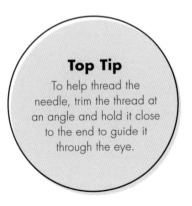

Top Tip

To help thread the needle, trim the thread at an angle and hold it close to the end to guide it through the eye.

Sewing on a button

"I can't even sew a button on!" is a popular claim that often follows any mention of sewing or garment care. Yet sewing a button back on is the ground zero of garment repair. Literally five minutes' effort can prevent an item from falling into permanent disuse.

You will need hand-sewing needle, thread, same-size buttons, scissors/thread snips

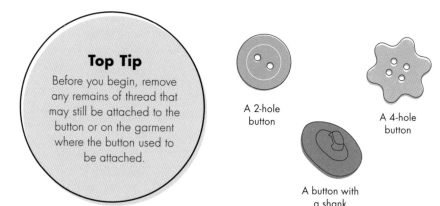

Top Tip

Before you begin, remove any remains of thread that may still be attached to the button or on the garment where the button used to be attached.

A 2-hole button

A 4-hole button

A button with a shank

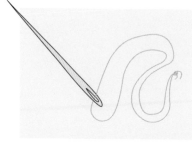

1 Thread a sewing needle with a strand of thread about 20 in (50 cm) long. Hold together both ends of the thread and tie a knot. Tie a second knot over the top of the first to make it bulkier. You now have a double thickness of thread. Next, follow the method appropriate for your type of button.

SEWING ON A BUTTON WITH HOLES

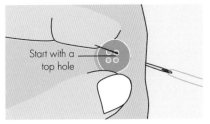

Start with a top hole

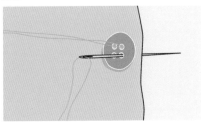

2a Push the needle through the fabric from behind and through a top hole. Hold the button in place while pulling the needle and thread all the way through.

3a Push the needle through the hole below and pull it and the thread all the way through. Repeat steps 2a and 3a three or four times; repeat for the second pair of holes, as necessary.

SEWING ON A SHANK BUTTON

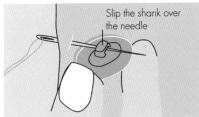

Slip the shank over the needle

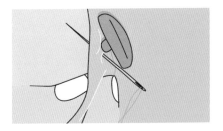

2b Push the needle through the fabric from behind and under the shank. Hold the button in place while pulling the needle and thread all the way through.

3b Keep the button flat against the garment. Push the needle through the fabric below the shank and pull it and the thread all the way through. Repeat steps 2b and 3b three or four times.

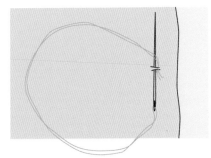

4 Flip the garment over so you can clearly see the area behind the button. Make two small stitches on top of each other, over the stitching that is holding your button on. Pull tight and trim the excess thread close to the fabric.

Repairing a buttonhole

Broken stitching around a buttonhole can lead to some annoying fraying. Not only does it look tatty, but it can also make it tricky to push the button through. Yet a few carefully placed stitches can repair that broken stitching, and bring an unrivaled feeling of satisfaction.

You will need scissors/thread snips, hand-sewing needle, color-matched thread

Left-handed? Work in the opposite direction to the one shown here if that feels more comfortable

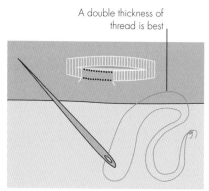

A double thickness of thread is best

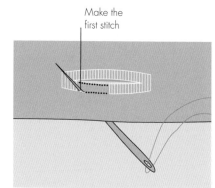

Make the first stitch

1 Carefully cut away any fraying and, if possible, remove the broken stitches from the original buttonhole. Refer to step 1 of Sewing on a button (p.30) for how to prepare the needle and thread.

2 Hold the garment so the right side is facing you and the buttonhole is lying horizontally. Push the needle up through the fabric from behind, coming out at the bottom of the original stitch height. Pull the needle and thread out from above.

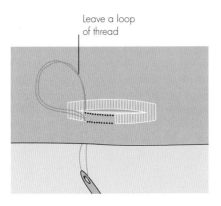

Leave a loop of thread

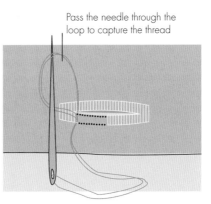

Pass the needle through the loop to capture the thread

3 Post the needle down through the slit of the buttonhole directly above where your needle emerged. Pull the needle and thread most of the way through the slit from behind. Pull gently, leaving a loop of thread on the right side.

4 Push the needle up through the fabric again from behind at the same point as step 2. Pull the needle and thread out from above, then pass the needle through the loop of thread from step 3. Pull the needle and thread upward to tighten.

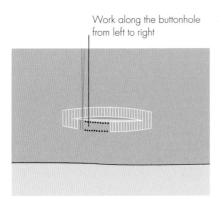

Work along the buttonhole from left to right

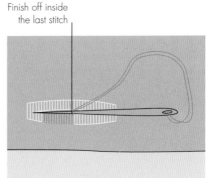

Finish off inside the last stitch

5 Post the needle through the slit as before, then push it through the fabric from behind, slightly to the right of the last stitch. Pull the needle and thread out almost all the way, leaving a loop, as before. Pass through this second loop and tighten.

6 Continue to repeat step 5, always pushing the needle up slightly to the right of the previous stitch, until the broken area has been filled in. To finish off, make one tiny stitch through the inner edge of the last stitch. Pull tightly and trim the thread.

Contrasting buttons

CHANGING THE BUTTONS IS AN EASY
WAY TO ALTER THE LOOK OF A GARMENT.
DO MAKE SURE THE NEW ONES ARE THE
SAME SIZE AS THE OLD ONES.

Repairing a hem

Mending a hem that has come undone is a simple task. If the original hem has barely visible stitches, follow the invisible-hem method (see opposite). If it has a visible row of stitches, use the visible-hem method (see pp.38–39). Color match the thread to the fabric for both methods.

You will need   **Invisible-hem method:** iron, ironing board, pins, tape measure, sharp hand-sewing needle, color-matched thread, scissors/thread snips
Visible-hem method: scissors/thread snips, pins (optional), hand-sewing needle, color-matched thread, fabric-marking tool (optional)

Left-handed?   Work in the opposite direction to the one shown here if that feels more comfortable

Top Tip

if the broken section of hem stitching is quite long, it's a good idea to use a fabric-marking tool to draw a stitching line to guide you.

Invisible-hem method

If the hem of your garment was originally sewn with barely visible stitching, use the slip-stitch method below to repair your hem and match it seamlessly.

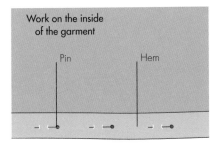

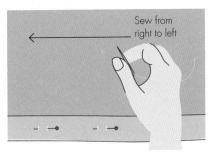

1 Using the original crease line as your guide, refold the section of loose hem and press the crease with an iron if necessary. Pin the hem in place, positioning the pins horizontally about ⅝in (1.5 cm) below the hem's inner edge, pointing left.

2 Thread a sharp needle with a single strand of thread no longer than 18 in (45 cm). Tie a knot at one end of the thread. Hold the garment so the folded edge of the hem is facing you and sew from right to left.

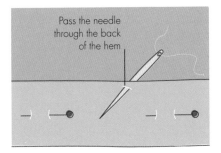

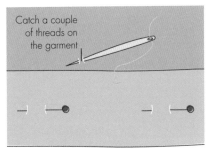

3 Secure the thread by passing the needle through the back of the hem to the front, about ³⁄₁₆in (5 mm) from the top edge, so that the knot is hidden behind the hem.

4 Make a stitch, no more than ⅜in (1 cm) long, diagonally to the left by catching a couple of threads of the fabric just above the hem. Pull the thread through to complete the stitch, but don't pull too tight. **»**

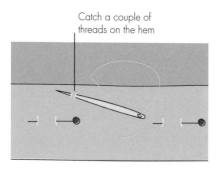

Catch a couple of
threads on the hem

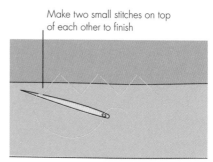

Make two small stitches on top
of each other to finish

5 Bring the tip of the needle diagonally down and to the left. Make another stitch, no more than ⅜in (1 cm) long, by catching a couple of threads of the hem fabric. Pull the thread through to complete the stitch. Continue in this way to reattach the hem.

6 To finish, remove the pins and make two small stitches, about ¾₆in (5 mm) long, on top of each other through the hem fabric only. Trim the excess sewing thread close to the fabric. Give your finished hem repair a gentle press with an iron to set the stitches.

- -

Visible-hem method

Mending a hem with visible stitching is even easier than with slip stitch! It's time to learn how to backstitch.

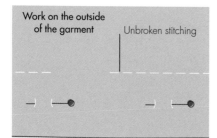

Work on the outside
of the garment   Unbroken stitching

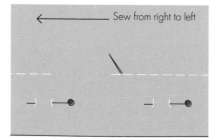

Sew from right to left

1 Carefully remove any remaining threads from the broken section of stitching. Position the hem with the outside of the garment facing up. If necessary, pin the broken section of hem back in place, positioning the pins horizontally.

2 Refer to step 1 of Sewing on a button (p.30) for how to prepare the needle and thread. Push the needle up in between the last two unbroken stitches of the original row of hem stitching. Pull the needle and thread out from the front.

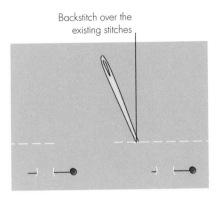

Backstitch over the existing stitches

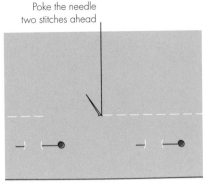

Poke the needle two stitches ahead

3 Take the needle backward, away from the section of broken stitching. Push the needle down through the fabric one stitch length away from where it emerged. Pull the needle and thread down from behind; these overlapping stitches should prevent it from unraveling.

4 Still holding the needle behind the hem, bring the needle back toward the broken section. Push the needle up through the fabric two stitch lengths to the left. Pull the needle and thread out from the front. Make another backstitch, one stitch length to the right.

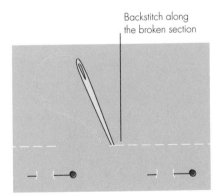

Backstitch along the broken section

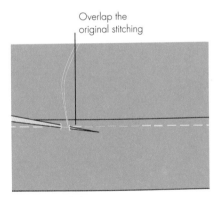

Overlap the original stitching

5 You have now made two stitches over the original stitching. Repeat step 4 to continue making backstitches along the broken section of hem. Remember to try to match your stitch length to the original hem stitching so your stitches blend in.

6 When your row of backstitches reaches the original stitching, complete two more stitches. Flip the hem over to the inside. To finish, remove the pins and make two small stitches on top of each other, behind a backstitch; these should not be visible from the front. Trim the excess thread.

Mending a hole from the top

View a hole in clothes as an opportunity to have some fun!
Patch over it; the effect can be subtle, beautiful, or bonkers.
Then, celebrate your repair with sashiko-style stitching.

Use this technique with patches and thread color-matched to the garment when repairing areas you might not wish to highlight—such as the seat of your jeans.

Alternatively, you can use a contrasting color of thread or the patch itself on the knees, elbows, and anywhere else you need a talking point.

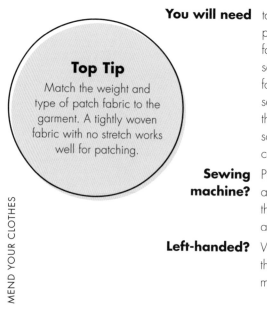

Top Tip

Match the weight and type of patch fabric to the garment. A tightly woven fabric with no stretch works well for patching.

You will need tape measure, fabric to make the patch or appliqué, fabric-marking tool, fabric scissors, iron, ironing board, safety pins (use dressmaking pins if the fabric is likely to be damaged by safety pins), hand-sewing needle, thread (color to match or contrast), scissors/thread snips, 100 percent cotton sashiko thread (optional)

Sewing machine? Prepare and secure the patch or appliqué as shown in steps 1 to 3, then try using a wide zigzag stitch around the edge of your shape

Left-handed? Work in the opposite direction to the one shown here if that feels more comfortable

1 Inspect the shape and position of the hole or holes, and check if the surrounding area is weakened or damaged at all. Decide on a shape for your patch; a simple rectangle or square will be easiest to begin with.

2 Measure how wide and deep the patch will need to be to cover the hole (and any damaged area, as necessary). Add an extra 1 in (2.5 cm) to each side and draw this bigger shape out on your patching fabric with a marking tool. You can make your patch larger if you wish.

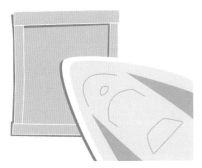

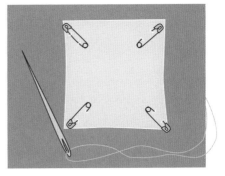

3 Cut the fabric shape out carefully. With the right side of your patch facing down, turn each edge in by ³⁄₈ in (1 cm) and press with an iron.

4 Position your patch centrally over the hole or damaged area and pin it in place. Thread a sewing needle with a strand of thread about 39 in (1 m) long as shown in step 1 on p.30. You now have a double thickness of thread. **»**

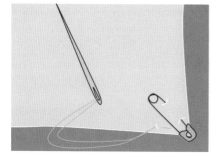

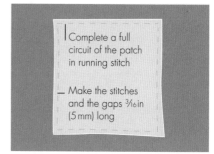

Complete a full circuit of the patch in running stitch

— Make the stitches and the gaps 3/16in (5mm) long

5 Start at a corner. From behind, push the needle up about 3/16in (5mm) from the edge of the patch. Pull the needle and thread through from the front then push it back down about 3/16in (5mm) to the left and repeat.

6 Repeat step 5 until you've stitched around all the edges. Keep stitches an even length and 3/16in (5mm) from the edge. From behind through the garment fabric only, make two small stitches on top of each other to finish. Trim the thread.

Basic sashiko-style stitching

For additional strength and beautification, why not try some sashiko-style stitching?

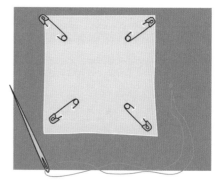

Top Tip

If you don't have sashiko thread, use two strands of regular thread and knot all four ends together (a four-ply thread).

1 Prepare your patch as in steps 1 to 3 on p.41. Using sashiko thread looks great, but a similar effect can be achieved with regular thread (see Top Tip, left) to sew with a four-ply thread. Use sashiko thread single ply with a knot in one end.

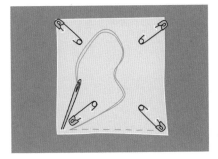

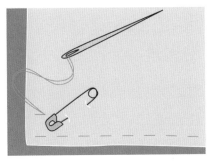

2 Follow step 5 (opposite) to complete one row of horizontal stitches. Try to keep the stitches even in length and finish your last stitch ³⁄₁₆ in (5 mm) from the edge of your patch.

3 From behind, bring the needle vertically above your last stitch. Push the needle up so it emerges ⅜ in (1 cm) above the end of your last stitch. Pull the needle and thread through from the front. Now stitch in the opposite direction to the previous row.

Now make
vertical stitches

4 Continue this second row of stitches, keeping each one ³⁄₁₆ in (5 mm) in length. Each stitch should be positioned directly above the previous row's stitches, ⅜ in (1 cm) apart. Continue adding rows of stitches in alternate directions until the patch is covered. Move the pins as necessary.

5 You can finish here, or continue to make a lovely cross/star effect. Push the needle up from behind ⅛ in (3 mm) above the center of the last stitch. Cross the stitch and push the needle down to make a vertical ³⁄₁₆ in (5 mm) stitch. Work down and up to "cross" all horizontal stitches.

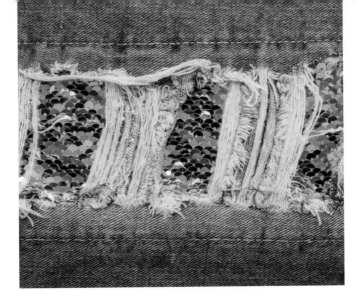

Visible mending

VISIBLE REPAIRS—PATCHED FROM
ABOVE OR BELOW—BROADCAST TO
THE WORLD THAT YOU ARE PROUD
TO EXTEND THE LIFE OF YOUR CLOTHES.

Patching a hole from behind

You've learned how to patch from the top (see pp.40–43), now let's add a few more hole-repair approaches to your repertoire. Patching a hole or damaged area from the inside gives you a more discreet fix while preventing the issue from getting worse. Here are three ways to do it.

You will need

Patching robust garments: scissors/thread snips, tape measure, fabric-marking tool, ruler (optional), fabric to make the patch (tightly woven fabrics with no stretch work best), fabric scissors, safety pins or pins, hand-sewing needle, thread, 100 percent cotton sashiko thread (optional)

No-sew method: scissors/thread snips, iron-on interfacing, iron, ironing board, pressing cloth

Stitching for strength: fabric-marking tool, tape measure, ruler (optional), iron-on interfacing, fabric scissors, iron, ironing board, pressing cloth, hand-sewing needle, color-matched thread or 100 percent cotton sashiko thread, scissors/thread snips

Sewing machine? Use for Stitching for strength (see p.51)

Left-handed? Work in the opposite direction to the one shown here if that feels more comfortable

Patching robust garments

Use this method to fix holes in robust garments—jeans, trousers, and unlined jackets. The colors of the patch and thread will help this repair either stand out or blend in.

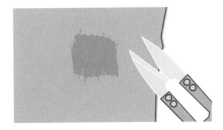

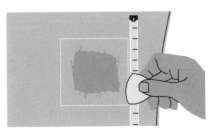

1 Lay the item right-side up and inspect the hole. Trim any threads from the hole's inner edge. Consider the patch's size and shape to cover the hole (and weakened area), then add ¾in (2 cm) or so all round.

2 With a fabric-marking tool, draw this shape directly onto the garment—it should cover the damaged area generously. Shapes with straight edges are easier to work with, so draw along a ruler or tape.

Position the patch fabric behind

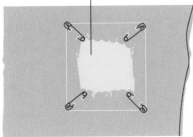

Start at a corner

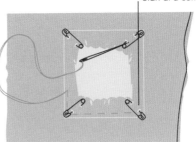

3 Using the shape you've drawn as a template, cut a patch out of scrap fabric that matches its size and shape. Position the patch on the inside so its outline matches the drawn shape. Pin in place.

4 Prepare a needle and thread as in step 1 on p.42. Push the needle up from behind ⅜in (1 cm) from the patch's edge. Sew running stitch around all edges, secure, and trim thread (see steps 5 and 6, p.42). **»**

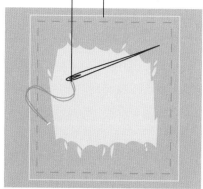

Use four-ply thread or sashiko thread

This running stitch keeps the patch in place

5 With some new thread, prepare your needle and thread as before. Now, you will create a whip stitch around the edge of the hole. Push the needle up from behind through both layers, about 3/16in (5 mm) from the edge of the hole. Pull the needle and thread through at the front.

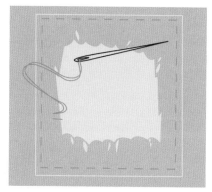

6 Push the needle back down just inside the edge of the hole into the patch fabric. Pull the needle and thread down at the back. For the next stitch, move the needle diagonally to one side and push it up again to the front, close to your first whip stitch. Pull the needle and thread through at the front.

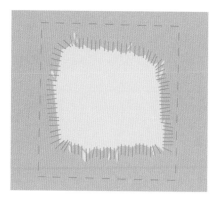

7 Continue to whip stitch all around the edge of the hole. To finish, take your needle to the back and make two small stitches on top of each other through the garment fabric only; they shouldn't be visible from the front. Trim the excess thread and remove any fabric marking.

No-sew method

This simple no-sew method is great for tackling very small holes, particularly on jersey garments and thinner fabrics.

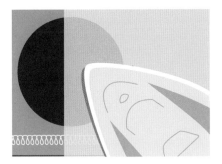 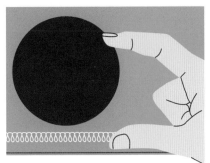

1 Choose an appropriate weight of iron-on interfacing and cut out a circle that will easily cover the hole. Position the circle, glue-side down, over the hole on the inside of the garment. Using a pressing cloth to avoid any glue (see Top Tip, below), press with the iron. The interfacing requires heat to stick, but check your garment can take the heat.

2 Check that the interfacing is properly applied: try picking at the edge with a fingernail. If the interfacing starts to come away, press down with the iron for longer or, if possible, increase the heat of the iron. Do be careful not to scorch the fabric!

Top Tip

Always use a pressing cloth between iron and interfacing or interfacing and ironing board to avoid getting glue in the wrong place. A light- or medium-weight 100 percent cotton fabric—an old, clean handkerchief or section of bedsheet—would work well as a pressing cloth.

Stitching for strength

Add the first and second methods together and you get this technique, which combines the stabilizing interfacing with extra stitching for strength—perfect for areas that get a lot of wear and tear but you don't wish to highlight.

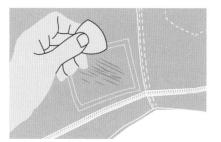

1 Lay out the garment and inspect the damaged or weakened area. Hold the fabric up to the light to see how far it extends. On the inside of the garment, draw a shape that will cover this area with a fabric-marking tool. Extend the shape by ¾ in (2 cm) on all sides.

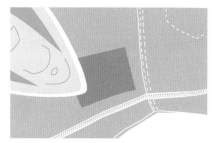

2 Choose a weight of iron-on interfacing that matches the thickness of the garment fabric (the undamaged part). Referring to the guide you made in step 1, cut the required shape out of the interfacing. Follow the No-sew method (see p.49) to apply the interfacing to the inside of the garment using an iron.

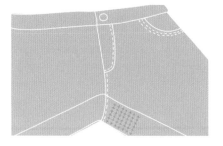

3 Thread a needle with sashiko thread, or prepare four-ply thread using regular thread as in step 1 on p.42 (see Top Tip). Try to use a thread that matches the color of your garment fabric as closely as possible. Turn the item right-side out and follow steps 2 to 5 (on p.43) to cover the damaged area with neat, sashiko-style cross stitches.

USING A SEWING MACHINE

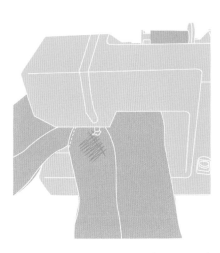

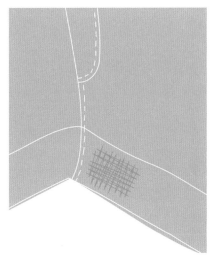

1 You can use a sewing machine instead of hand stitching for step 3. Set up the machine (see also pp.26–29). Locate the stitch type selector and choose a straight stitch. Then select 3–3.5 on the stitch length selector.

2 Position the item on the machine (which can be tricky depending where the patch is) and stitch back and forth over the damaged area. Turn the garment so that you next stitch at right angles to the first row of stitches to strengthen the repair.

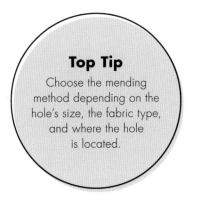

Top Tip
Choose the mending method depending on the hole's size, the fabric type, and where the hole is located.

Darning a hole

Discovering a hole in your favorite sweater or knitted garment can be sad, but it needn't spell the end. Hole-darning is a little more time consuming than other repairs in this book, but channeling your inner grandma is really worth it to extend the life of your clothes.

You will need darning needle, darning yarn (choose a close color match for a repair that will blend in or a contrast color to create a visible repair), scissors/thread snips, darning mushroom or egg (or base of a drinking glass or orange) (optional)

Left-handed? Work in the opposite direction to the one shown here if that feels more comfortable

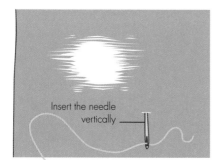

Insert the needle vertically

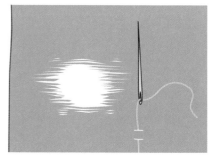

1 Thread a darning needle with a strand of darning yarn about 20 in (50 cm) long. Leave the end unknotted. With the item right-side up (with a darning mushroom beneath), insert the point of the needle about ⅝ in (1.5 cm) away from the hole.

2 Hold the needle at the front of the garment throughout. Push the point of the needle out again, ⅛ in (4 mm) from where it was inserted. Pull the needle and thread out and upward from above, but leave a tail of thread about 1⅝ in (4 cm) long.

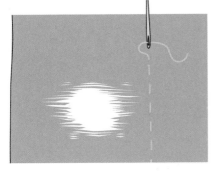

Where there's no fabric, long stitches span the hole

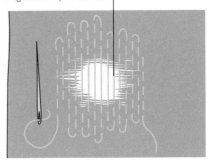

3 Continue to weave the needle in and out of the fabric, making a row of running stitches. Try to keep the stitches small and even, no more than ⅛ in (4 mm) in length. Continue until the row extends at least ⅝ in (1.5 cm) above the hole.

4 At the end of the row, leave a tiny loop of yarn, change direction, and sew another row of running stitches, close to the first but heading downward. Continue to go up and down in this way to cover the whole area. The tiny loops of yarn at the end of rows allow for shrinkage.

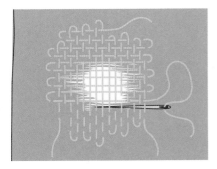

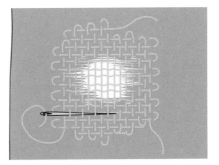

5 Make horizontal rows of running stitch, weaving in and out of the vertical stitches when over the hole. This will create a new "fabric" over the hole. Don't worry if it doesn't look dense over the hole, as the darning yarn will become fuzzy through wear and bulk out.

6 During the repair, it is likely that you will need to rethread your needle with more yarn, and by the end there will be loose threads around the edge of the darning. Take each loose end in turn, thread it on to your needle, and weave it into the repair to hide and secure it.

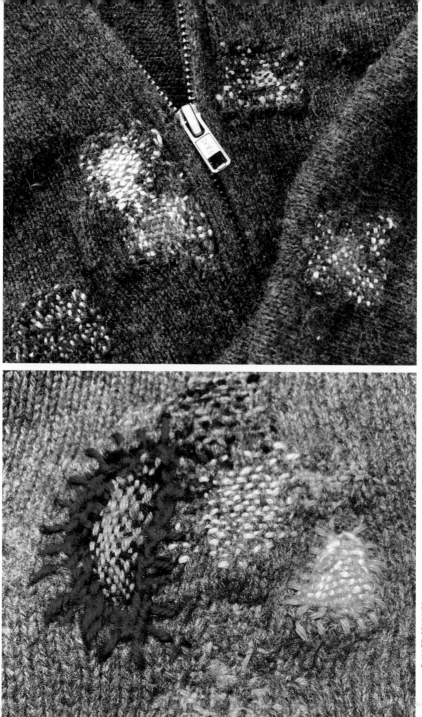

© KATE SEKULES

Visible darning

MENDING KNITWEAR OFFERS A GREAT
OPPORTUNITY TO HAVE FUN. DON'T
BOTHER TRYING TO MATCH COLORS—ADD
A CONTRAST COLOR POP INSTEAD.

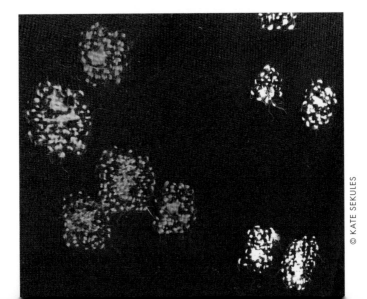

© KATE SEKULES

Mending a tear

By this point, you've got a few tricks up your sleeve for dealing with holes in your garment. But what if that sleeve has a tear or a rip in it? Fear not, here are two more tricks.

You will need　**Robust repair:** iron-on interfacing, fabric scissors, iron, ironing board, pressing cloth, hand-sewing needle, color-matched thread, scissors/thread snips

Less-visible repair: pins, fabric-marking tool, hand-sewing needle, color-matched thread, scissors/thread snips, iron, ironing board

Sewing machine?　**Robust repair:** follow steps 1 and 2, then use a wide zigzag stitch over the tear instead of the whip stitch

Less-visible repair: follow steps 1 and 2, then use a straight stitch (set to length 2) instead of the running stitch

Top Tip

If the area around a tear is damaged, you may need to patch it (see pp.40–49). If it's just a rip or tear, use one of the methods shown here.

Robust repair

Let's revisit and redeploy the whip stitch (see p.48). Although more visible than the next method, this method creates a more stable, secure repair for garments that get a lot of use.

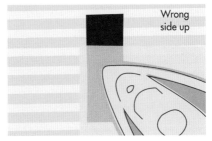

1 Choose iron-on interfacing of a similar weight to the fabric of your garment; it will stabilize the torn area ahead of stitching. Cut out a rectangle about 1 in (2.5 cm) wide and 1 in (2.5 cm) longer than the tear.

2 Place the garment wrong side up on an ironing board. Butt the edges of the tear together and position the interfacing (glue-side down) over the tear. Using a pressing cloth, carefully press with an iron.

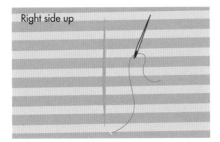

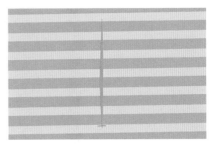

3 With the right side up, prepare your needle and thread as in step 2 on p.37. Starting just below and at least ⅛in (3 mm) to the side of the tear, push the needle up from behind and pull it out from the front.

4 Take the needle across to the other side of the tear. Push it through the fabric to make a stitch that straddles the tear. Pull the needle and thread down from behind. Don't pull too tightly to avoid "pinching." **»**

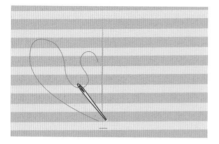

5 From behind, take the needle diagonally upward. Push the needle up through the interfacing and the fabric, this time about ⅛in (3 mm) above the first stitch. Pull the needle and thread out from the front. Repeat step 4 to complete stitch two.

6 Repeat steps 4 and 5 to create an even "ladder" of stitches along the length of the tear. Make one or two extra stitches beyond the end of the tear. Then, from the back make two small stitches on top of each other. Trim the excess thread.

Less-visible repair

Running stitch helps create a less-visible mend (great for patterned fabric, less so for fabrics that fray).

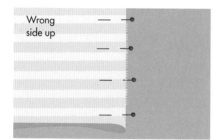

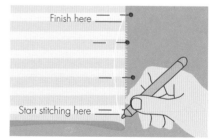

1 Fold the garment with the right sides facing so that the length of the tear runs along the folded edge. Keep the fabric flat and in position by placing pins perpendicular to the fold.

2 With the item flat, draw a guide for the stitching—a smooth, curved line that runs about ³⁄₁₆in (5 mm) from the edge of the tear—with a fabric-marking tool. Start and finish about ⅜in (1 cm) from each end.

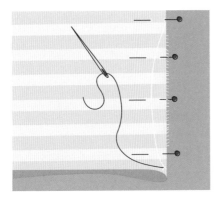

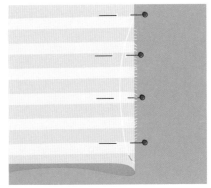

3 Prepare your needle and thread as in step 2 on p.37. Starting very close to the folded edge, push the needle up from behind through both layers of fabric. Pull the needle and thread out from the front.

4 Push the needle back down about ⅛ in (3 mm) further along the line. Pull the needle and thread down from behind. The aim is for tight stitches, but try to keep the fabric flat and avoid puckering.

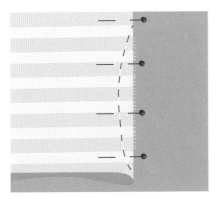

Turn the fabric over and iron on the right side

5 Push the needle to the front about ⅛ in (3 mm) from the first stitch and continue with neat, even running stitch along the line. Check often that the stitches pass through unbroken fabric and are at least ³⁄₁₆ in (5 mm) from the edge of the tear.

6 When the row of stitching returns to the folded edge, make two small stitches on top of each other to finish. Trim the excess thread and remove the pins. Turn the garment around and, with the iron on a low setting, gently press the repair flat.

Mending a split seam

A split seam differs from a tear because only the stitching is broken; the fabric is still intact. If a split seam is the issue, even if the garment is fully lined, it is easy to create an invisible-to-the-naked-eye repair.

You will need
Repair from the top: scissors/thread snips, hand-sewing needle, color-matched thread
Repair from the inside: scissors/thread snips, pins (optional), hand-sewing needle, color-matched thread, fabric-marking tool (optional)
Repair and reinforcement: scissors/thread snips, tape measure, iron-on interfacing, fabric scissors, iron, ironing board, pressing cloth, fabric-marking tool, hand-sewing needle, color-matched thread

Sewing machine?
Repair from the inside: follow steps 1 and 2 and then use a straight stitch instead of the running stitch.
Repair and reinforcement: follow steps 1 to 4 and then use a straight stitch instead of running stitch

Left-handed? Work in the opposite direction to the one shown here if that feels more comfortable

Repair from the top

Mend any split seam by creating a version of the slip stitch
(also known as ladder stitch, invisible stitch, or blind stitch)
that we first used to repair a hem (see pp.36–38).

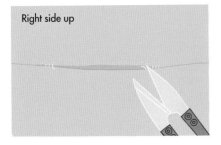

Right side up

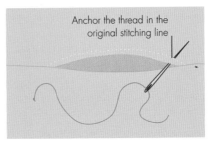

Anchor the thread in the
original stitching line

1 With the right side facing you, snip any
loose threads in the split. Thread a needle
with a length of thread about 12 in (30 cm)
long. Tie a knot in one end, then tie a
second knot over the first to make it bulkier.

2 Insert the needle through the seam
allowance on the inside of the split so
that its point emerges on the original seam
where the split begins. Pull the needle out
from the front, so the knot stays hidden.

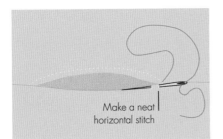

Make a neat
horizontal stitch

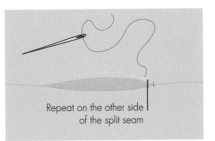

Repeat on the other side
of the split seam

3 Bring the needle across the seam
directly below where it emerged. Insert
the needle into the opposite edge of the
original seam and take it across to the left,
making a horizontal stitch ⅛ in (3 mm) long.

4 Pull the needle and thread to start to
close the gap between the seam edges.
Take the needle back across the seam and
make a ⅛ in- (3 mm-) long horizontal stitch in
the seam's upper edge. **»**

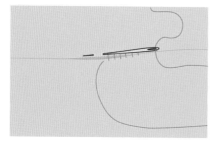

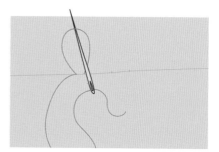

5 Repeat steps 3 and 4 along the length of the split seam. Carefully pull the thread at the end of each stitch tightly enough to close the gap but avoiding puckering. You want invisible stitches with a nice flat seam.

6 To finish, make a tiny stitch just inside the edge of the seam. Pull the thread through gently, leaving a little loop of thread. Pass the needle through this loop, then pull tightly and trim the excess thread.

Repair from the inside

Use this method to repair a split seam in an unlined garment where you can access both sides of the split stitching—it makes for a robust and long-lasting repair.

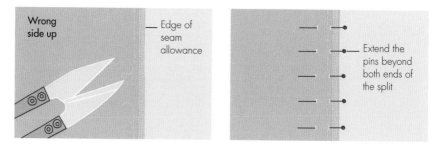

Wrong side up

— Edge of seam allowance

Extend the pins beyond both ends of the split

1 Lay the garment down on a flat surface so the inside of the garment is facing up and the seam is visible. Carefully cut away any loose threads from both sides of the split section of seam.

2 Unless the split section is very short, use pins to stabilize it and keep it flat while you work. Insert the pins perpendicular to the seam. Prepare a needle and thread as in step 1 on p.61.

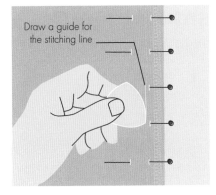

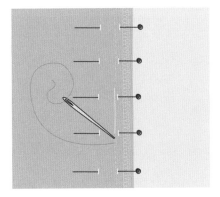

3 To fill in the split section you will use a running stitch along the original seam line. If the crease or the holes created by the original stitching aren't visible, draw a guide using a fabric-marking tool.

4 Start a few stitches into the unbroken section of the seam. Push the needle up from behind through both layers of fabric and then push back down about ⅛ in (3 mm) further on and pull down from behind.

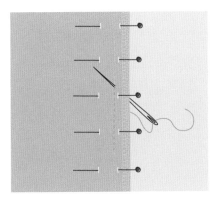

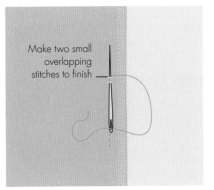

5 Repeat step 4 to make a row of running stitches that fills in the split section. Take care to keep your stitches on the original seam line. Make a couple of extra stitches that overlap with the original unbroken stitching.

6 To finish, make two small stitches on top of each other over your final stitch. Trim the excess thread and remove any pins. With the iron on a low setting, gently press the seam flat from the reverse side.

Repair and reinforcement

When stress has been put on a seam, a split in the stitching may be accompanied by fraying or damage to the fabric. This method deals with both issues and offers a neat finish.

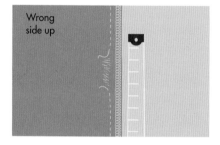

1 Lay the garment down on a flat surface so the inside of the garment is facing up and the seam is visible. Carefully cut away any loose threads. Measure the length of the split and damaged section.

2 Select a fusible interfacing of a similar weight to your garment. Add an extra 1 in (2.5 cm) to the length of the split you measured and mark out a shape ⅝ in (1.5 cm) wide. Cut out two strips this size.

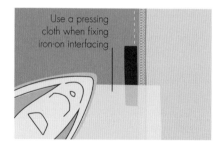

3 Position one strip of interfacing centrally over the area of split seam and damaged fabric, glue-side down. Using a pressing cloth, fix with an iron. Flip the seam over and repeat with the second strip.

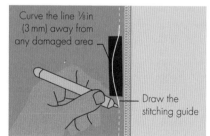

4 Draw a stitching guide with a fabric-marking tool. Start on the original stitching line, then curve about ⅛ in (3 mm) away from any fraying so the stitching goes through undamaged fabric. Rejoin the line.

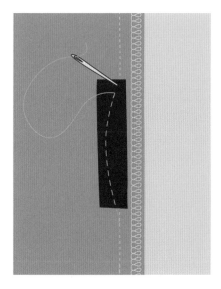

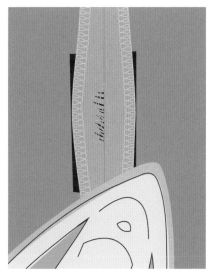

5 Prepare the needle and thread as in step 2 on p.37, then repeat steps 4 to 6 on p.63 to make a row of running stitches. To avoid unraveling, make a few stitches that overlap the original stitching at the start and finish of the new stitched line.

6 Press the repaired seam on the inside of the garment—if it's an open seam, press the seam apart; if it's a closed seam, press both parts of the seam together to one side. Then, flip the item over and press the repair from the front.

Top Tip

Match the weight and shade of the iron-on interfacing to that of the garment fabric for the best finish.

Zipper issues

Zippers are ingenious inventions, and it's tricky to imagine a wardrobe without them. However, they can malfunction in numerous—and spectacular—ways. Replacing a zipper is best left to a tailor or alterations expert, but here are some tips and tricks that are worth trying at home first.

There are three main types of zippers found in clothing: open-ended, closed-ended, and concealed/invisible. The ends of open-end zippers can be separated completely and are mainly used to fasten zip-through hoodies and jackets. Closed-end zippers are joined at the base. These are found in various types of garments, including the fly fronts of jeans and trousers. Concealed (or invisible) zippers are almost exclusively found in womenswear. When inserted well, only the zipper pull is visible, so it helps a garment maintain a sleek, well-fitting silhouette.

Metal or plastic?

Most modern zippers have plastic teeth made from polyester or nylon. The teeth in lightweight, plastic-toothed zippers are formed from a coil. On the other hand, metal zippers, often found in jeans and more robust outerwear, have separate teeth made from brass, stainless steel, aluminum, or zinc.

The anatomy of a closed-end zipper

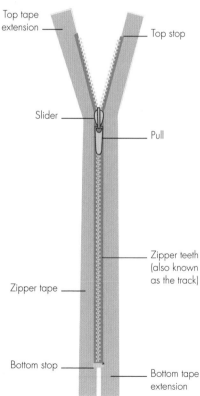

Top tape extension

Top stop

Slider

Pull

Zipper teeth (also known as the track)

Zipper tape

Bottom stop

Bottom tape extension

FREE UP A STICKY ZIPPER

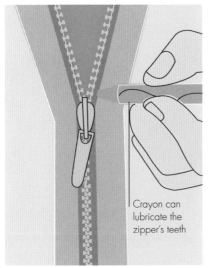

Crayon can lubricate the zipper's teeth

A PAPER CLIP TURNED PULL

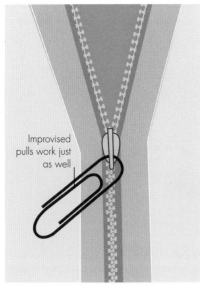

Improvised pulls work just as well

A sticky zipper

It can be infuriating when a zipper is sticking. If your zipper is difficult to open and close, first check to see if something's caught in the teeth: a hair or thread, perhaps. Otherwise, some lubrication along the teeth just above or below the slider may be in order. Candle wax, crayon, pencil lead, soap, or lip balm can help coax a zipper back into action. Then, jiggle the slider to work the lubricant into the teeth. Just be careful not to stain the fabric of your garment.

A broken or missing zipper pull

It can be super-fussy to open and close your zipper if the zipper pull breaks off. But if the loop on the front of the slider is still intact, you're in luck. Try threading a thin piece of wire through this loop and making a ring to act as a new zipper pull. A paper clip or key ring can also work for this. You can also source fancier replacement zipper pulls.

TIGHTEN A ZIPPER SLIDER

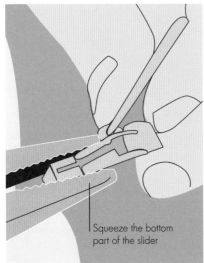

Squeeze the bottom part of the slider

HELP THE ZIPPER STAY UP

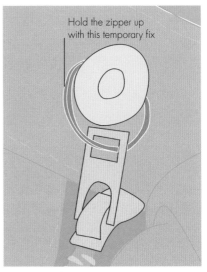

Hold the zipper up with this temporary fix

MEND A HOLE BELOW A ZIPPER

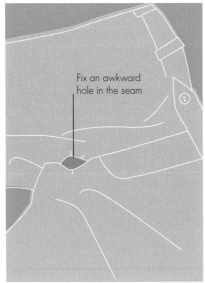

Fix an awkward hole in the seam

REMOVE A BROKEN SLIDER

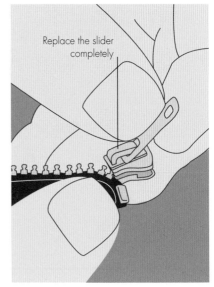

Replace the slider completely

A loose zipper slider

You have a loose zipper slider when it leaves some teeth open when you pull the zipper closed. A gentle squeeze with some pliers to the bottom part of the slider where it meets the teeth usually does the trick. Test the repaired zipper, and squeeze a little more, if necessary.

Hole in the seam below a zipper

The stress of repeatedly opening and closing a zipper can result in a hole appearing in the seam just below the zipper. This is particularly common in skirts and dresses with a concealed (or invisible) zipper. Follow the technique for method 1 of Mending a split seam on pp.60–62 to mend such a hole using a ladder stitch.

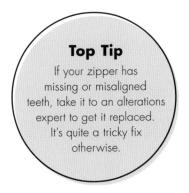

Top Tip

If your zipper has missing or misaligned teeth, take it to an alterations expert to get it replaced. It's quite a tricky fix otherwise.

A zipper won't stay up

Everyone can relate to the embarrassment associated with a fly mishap. If the zipper on your trousers or jeans refuses to stay closed, the long-term solution is to get the zipper replaced. But, a temporary measure is to attach a key-ring loop to the zipper pull. Pull the zipper closed, then hook this ring over the button on the waistband before fastening it to avoid any unwelcome fresh air or awkward encounters.

A broken zipper slider

Before taking the drastic (and more expensive) step of getting the entire zipper replaced, it's worth trying a little garment DIY since replacement zipper sliders can be bought cheaply online. Remove the broken slider by snipping it with a pair of wire cutters. At the top of the zipper on the same side that you removed the broken slider from, fold aside the top stop then slide the replacement slider onto the teeth and zip as normal.

Repairing collars and cuffs

After some years of use, a shirt or blouse can start to show signs of wear on the collar and cuffs while the rest of the garment still looks great. If only there was some way to reinforce and disguise these sad, worn-out areas. Oh, but there is! Enter: bias tape.

You will need tape measure, 39 in (1 m) or 1 pack of ¾ in (2 cm) wide or slightly wider bias tape (depending how it's sold), scissors/ thread snips, pins, hand-sewing needle, thread (match color to bias tape)

Left-handed? Work in the opposite direction to the one shown here if that feels more comfortable

Top Tip

You can find bias tape in a wide range of colors and patterns. Choose a close color match to the fabric of your garment for a subtle repair, or pick a contrasting bias tape that will add an entirely new design feature—it's up to you.

Fixing a collar

Collars rub against the neck, so over time the fabric starts to wear out. Whip stitching a length of bias tape along a collar will offer protection and extend a garment's life.

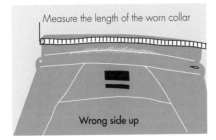

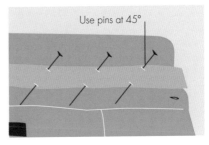

1 Lay the collar flat. Measure from edge to edge along the inner worn part. Trim the end of the bias tape if it isn't neat. Then, add ¾ in (2 cm) to the collar measurement and cut that length of bias tape.

2 Position the bias tape along the collar, centered over the worn part; ⅜ in (1 cm) will extend at each end. Pin it in place with pins at 45°. Prepare a needle and thread as in step 2 on p.37.

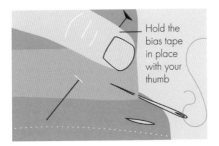

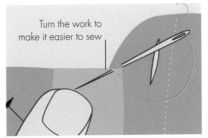

3 Fold under the end of the bias tape by ⅜ in (1 cm) to create a fold flush with the edge of the collar. Push the needle up through the bias tape at the bottom of the fold right at the edge, so the knot is hidden.

4 Push the point of the needle into the top layer of collar fabric, then push it diagonally across so it comes through the edge of the binding, about ⅛ in (3 mm) away from where it first emerged. »

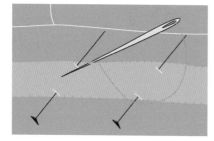

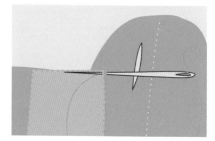

5 Continue making tiny whip stitches along the end and then the top length of the bias tape. When you reach the end, turn the collar around, fold over and stitch the short end, and finish the other length.

6 Push the needle up through the bias tape, then make a tiny stitch through the collar and tape. Pull it through, leaving a little loop of thread. Pass the needle through this loop, then pull tightly. Trim the thread.

- -

Mending cuffs

Apply bias tape to garment cuffs to transform them from tattered into toughened.

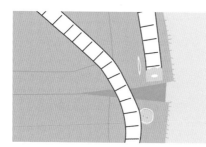

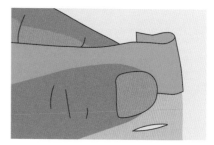

1 Measure the length of the cuff along the worn edge. Trim the end of the bias tape if it isn't neat, then add ¾ in (2 cm) to the cuff measurement and cut that length of bias tape.

2 Center the bias tape along the top edge of the cuff; it should extend by ⅜ in (1 cm) at each end. At one end, fold this extra bias tape to the back and keep it in place with your thumb and forefinger.

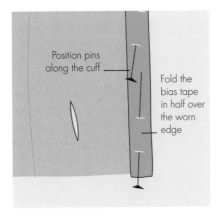

Position pins along the cuff

Fold the bias tape in half over the worn edge

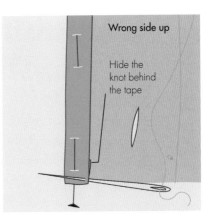

Wrong side up

Hide the knot behind the tape

3 Now, start to fold the bias tape in half lengthwise so that just half its width is visible. Pin the bias tape in place. Fold the second end of tape in, then fold and pin the remaining length of bias tape.

4 Prepare your needle and thread as in step 2 on p.37. Turn the cuff over and work on the inside now. Push the needle up through the folded edges of bias tape at the end of the cuff, so the knot is hidden.

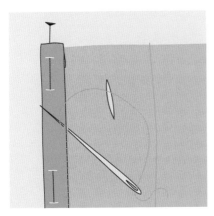

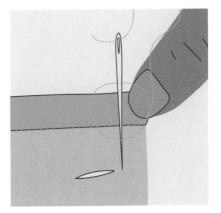

5 Repeat step 4 on p.57 to make the first whip stitch. Continue to make a row of whip stitches along the edge of the bias tape. Try to catch only the top layer of fabric of the cuff with your needle.

6 At the end of that row, push the needle through all layers of bias tape and cuff. Turn the cuff back to work on the outside. Continue to whip stitch the bias tape in place. Finish as in step 6 (opposite).

Repairing visible topstitching

Topstitching is the visible stitching that strengthens durable areas and highlights design features. When that stitching breaks, it can spoil the look of the garment. Allow our friend—the backstitch—to come to the rescue.

You will need   scissors/thread snips, pins (optional), hand-sewing needle, thread (color-matched topstitching thread or regular thread)

Sewing machine?   Prep the repair as in step 1 and select a straight stitch on the machine. Test the stitch on a scrap of fabric, then adjust the length of the stitch and retest until your stitching matches that of the original topstitching

Left-handed?   Work in the opposite direction to the one shown here if that feels more comfortable

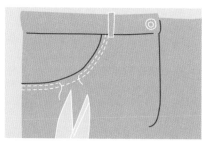

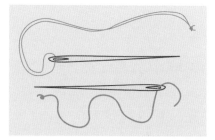

1 Carefully cut away any loose threads from the broken section of topstitching. If the topstitching secured a pocket or other feature that is now loose or out of position, use pins to keep it in place during stitching.

2 If using topstitching thread, thread the needle as in step 2 p.37. If using regular thread, use a strand 30 in (75 cm) long. Tie both ends in a knot (so it's double thickness) then tie a second knot.

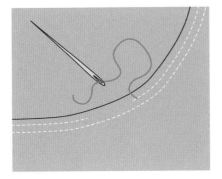

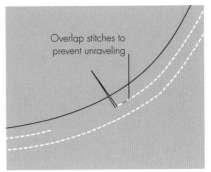

Overlap stitches to prevent unraveling

3 Use backstitch to fill in the gap of broken topstitching. From the inside, push the needle up between the last two unbroken stitches of the original row of topstitching. Pull the needle and thread through from the front.

4 Take the needle backward (away from the broken section) by one stitch. Push the needle down through the fabric overlapping the unbroken stitch and bring it up two stitch lengths to the left.

Try to match your stitch length to the original to blend in

Overlap by two stitches to secure

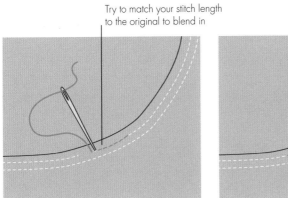

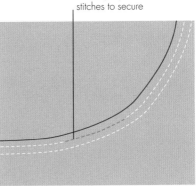

5 Make another backstitch, one stitch length to the right. Continue to backstitch along the broken section of topstitching. Match the stitch length of the original topstitching as much as possible.

6 When your backstitching fills the gap, overlap the unbroken stitches by two stitches. Push the needle to the back and on the inside make two small stitches on top of each other. Trim excess thread.

Visible stitching

TOPSTITCHING IS USED TO HIGHLIGHT AND STRENGTHEN SEAM LINES AND DESIGN DETAILS, AND CAN BE EASILY REPAIRED.

Wear Your Clothes

Introduction

What do you do with those clothes that aren't damaged and don't need fixing, but you hardly ever or never wear? This chapter shares heaps of ideas and the necessary know-how to rework garments into your new fave outfits.

Each and every garment in your wardrobe can be as unique as you are. And this section of the book offers plenty of inspiration and technical wizardry so that you can make this happen.

What's the problem?

How many garments in your wardrobe right now fit this description: there's nothing glaringly "wrong" with it but you just don't want to wear it any more? The hem is intact, the zipper doesn't stick, and there aren't any holes or split seams to fix. You used to like it—after all, at some point you decided to make it yours. And maybe the two of you had a delightful first few wears together. But for some reason, nowadays, it always gets passed over when you're getting dressed. It is no longer functioning as a piece of clothing, it has become "wardrobe filler," and its only apparent role now is to make it harder for you to find what you want.

Think sustainably

You could, of course, just take or send that garment to a secondhand store. Yet only a small fraction of donated clothing gets resold as clothing. Most is exported to foreign markets or sold on to be turned into rags.

Being sustainable and following slow fashion is about considering all the energy, resources, and labor that go into making a garment, and it's oh-so much better to address what's wrong in the first place.

Find time to get creative, flex your developing sewing skills, and breathe new life into unloved garments.

The evolution of a garment needn't stop where the designers and garment workers left off.

Give garments a second chance

Sometimes it's clear what you don't like about a garment: the fit is a bit frumpy, the hem scrapes along the floor, or there's just no pocket for your phone. Yet with others it can be harder to diagnose the problem (or problems). Perhaps the reason is more esthetic than practical, and therefore the issues feel more abstract. Discovering fresh ideas and approaches that other people have used can often spark an idea of how you could revitalize a garment or two in your wardrobe.

It seems a shame to call it quits with a garment simply because it feels somewhat "meh." Find time to get creative, flex your developing sewing skills, and breathe new life into those unloved garments.

A small tweak or a bigger transformation?

Perhaps you will choose to shorten those trousers by ¾in (2 cm) so they hit the ankle in *just* the right place. Or you might try lengthening that knee-length skirt to a midi by adding a striking contrast ruffle. Either way, this range of altering and reworking ideas may just help you feel excited about wearing an item of clothing again.

Do note that you don't have to stick to one reworking per garment. Got a slightly plain shirt dress? Why not add some waist-shaping darts and swap all the buttons for something more fun? Got an overly loose tunic top that seems to drown you? What about adding elastic at the cuffs and refitting it at the side seams? Got a practical jacket in your favorite color but the sleeves are a tad tight? You could turn it into a vest by removing the sleeves. Oh, and while you're there, you could add a pocket that will actually fit your hand.

A wardrobe that feels more "you"

Deploying a few clever fixes and techniques can make any garment feel more "you." The evolution of a garment needn't stop where the designers and garment workers left off. With these ideas and techniques under your belt, you are free to customize and personalize your clothing to fit your shape, style, and requirements.

Shortening a hem

It's no surprise that an off-the-rack garment's hem length won't always be exactly right. Shortening hems is an easy task; sometimes, an adjustment of just ¾in (2 cm) can make all the difference.

Top Tip

More dramatic transformations are also possible—turning long sleeves into short sleeves, jeans into shorts, or a dress into a top.

You will need pins, tape measure, fabric-marking tool, fabric scissors, iron, hand-sewing needle, color-matched thread, scissors/thread snips

Sewing machine? For hemming in step 6: for visible hems on a woven garment, use a straight stitch; for hems on knit/jersey garments, use a three-step zigzag

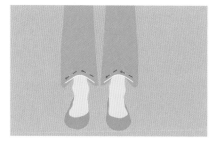

1 Try the garment on in front of a mirror and put on suitable footwear. Turn up a section of the hem to the desired length and roughly pin in place. Stand up to assess the new length; adjust if necessary.

2 Lay the garment right-side facing out on a flat surface. Based on the section you pinned, place a new pin horizontally to indicate what will be the bottom of the new finished length. Remove any other pins.

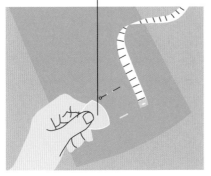

Mark the new length including its hem allowance

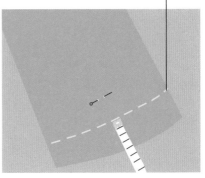

Measure up from the bottom to draw a consistent new hemline

3 Mark horizontally on the fabric below the pin what you'll need for a hem allowance. Add 1⅝ in (4 cm) for woven fabrics to hide the raw edge; add only ¾ in (2 cm) for knit/jersey as they don't fray.

4 Measure from the original hemline to the new mark. Measure up this amount from the bottom edge all around the hem, making horizontal marks on the fabric every 2 in (5 cm). Cut off the excess fabric.

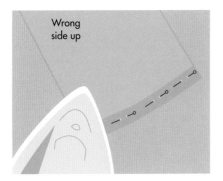

Wrong side up

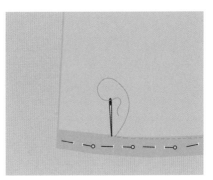

5 Turn the garment inside out. Turn up the bottom edge by ¾ in (2 cm), press, then pin. If the garment is woven, turn another ¾ in (2 cm) to hide the raw edge within the folded hem, and press again.

6 For woven fabrics, slip stitch as for an invisible hem (see pp.37–38); for a visible hem, use running stitch (see p.42). For a knit/jersey item, use a loose running stitch to allow stretching. Press the bottom edge.

Lengthening a hem

Sadly, we can't wave a magic wand to make a hem that feels too short grow longer. But we can attach a contrasting band of fabric to add length and create a cool design feature at the same time.

You will need

Adding a contrast band: tape measure, seam ripper, fabric-marking tool, fabric for contrast band, fabric scissors, pins, iron, ironing board, hand-sewing needle, thread (match color to the contrast fabric), scissors/thread snips

Creating a ruffle: tape measure, seam ripper, fabric-marking tool, fabric scissors, fabric for ruffle, pins, hand-sewing needle, thread (match color to the contrast fabric), iron, ironing board, scissors/thread snips

Sewing machine?

For hemming in steps 3 and 4 (p.87): for visible hems on a woven garment, use a straight stitch; for hems on knit/jersey garments, use a three-step zigzag. For attaching the band or ruffle in steps 6 (pp.86 and 87), use a straight stitch instead of a running stitch

Adding a contrast band

This method suits straight and A-line-shaped garments made from fabric that doesn't have much drape. Match the fabric for lengthening to the type and thickness of the garment.

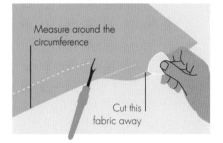

Measure around the circumference

Cut this fabric away

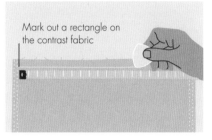

Mark out a rectangle on the contrast fabric

1 Try the item on and work out how much extra length you want. Measure around its bottom edge (circumference), unpick the original hem, and mark ⅜in (1 cm) below its bottom edge. Cut the fabric on this line.

2 Mark out a rectangle where the long sides match the item's circumference plus a ¾in (2 cm) seam allowance. If the contrast fabric is not wide enough, then join two rectangles of equal length.

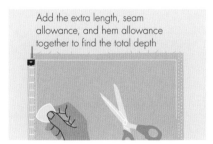

Add the extra length, seam allowance, and hem allowance together to find the total depth

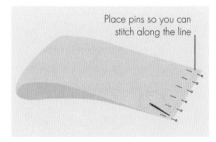

Place pins so you can stitch along the line

3 The depth of the rectangle is your extra length plus ⅜in (1 cm) seam allowance for the top edge, plus a hem allowance along the bottom edge (1⅝in/4 cm for woven fabric; ¾in/2 cm for knit/jersey). Cut out.

4 Lay the short ends of the rectangle on top of each other, with right sides facing, and pin. Sew the ends together using a running stitch ⅜in (1 cm) from the edge. Remove the pins and press the seam open. Follow steps 5 and 6 on p.83 to finish the bottom edge. **»**

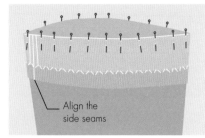

Align the
side seams

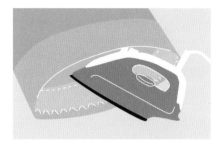

5 With the item upside down and the contrast band inside out, slip the contrast band over the garment. Align the side seams of the band with those of your garment. Pin to keep sections together.

6 Join the garment and band with a row of running stitches ⅜ in (1 cm) from the edge. Flip the contrast band down into position, then press the seam allowances at the join toward the garment on the inside.

Creating a ruffle

A romantic ruffle works equally well on straight or flared garments in light- to medium-weight fabrics.

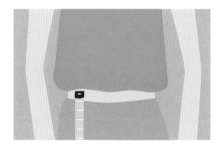

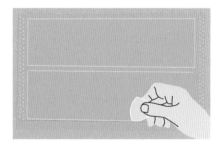

1 Follow step 1 on p.85 to measure and prepare your garment for lengthening. If the original hem is less than ⅜ in (1 cm) deep, there is no need to unpick. Note: a ruffle will require more fabric than a band.

2 Mark the rectangle for the ruffle. The long sides need to be 1½–2 times the circumference of your garment's hem, depending on how full a ruffle you'd like. Follow step 3 on p.85 for its depth.

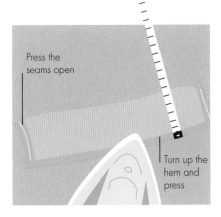

Press the
seams open

Turn up the
hem and
press

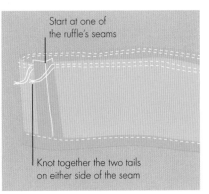

Start at one of
the ruffle's seams

Knot together the two tails
on either side of the seam

3 If the fabric isn't wide enough, divide the width into two equal rectangles. Follow step 4 on p.85 to stitch the short ends together and press the seams open. Turn up a hem to finish the ruffle's bottom edge.

4 Stitch two rows of long running stitches, the first ½in (1.3 cm) from the top edge, the other at ¼in (7 mm); leave long tails of thread at each end. Take a pair of tails and double knot them together.

Ease the fabric; the
gathers appear here

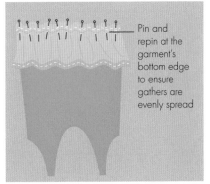

Pin and
repin at the
garment's
bottom edge
to ensure
gathers are
evenly spread

5 Hold one set of knotted-together tails tightly with one hand. With the other hand, gently ease the fabric along the threads, away from the tails. Continue until the gathered edge of the ruffle matches the circumference of your garment.

6 Tie all the loose tails together. Then, spread the gathers out evenly around the circumference. Follow steps 5 and 6 opposite to attach the ruffle; it just covers the gathering stitches. Once the ruffle is attached, remove the gathering stitches.

Contrast bands, trims, and ruffles

COLOR-BLOCKED BANDS, ROMANTIC RUFFLES, AND SWEET TRIMS CAN ALL LENGTHEN SLEEVES AND HEMS.

Adding a simple patch pocket

Garments that have no pockets, or pockets that are too small to actually use, are highly annoying. But what if you could just make your own pocket and add it on? Let's work through the steps of this real-life magic trick.

You will need a sheet of paper, pencil, ruler, paper scissors, fabric to make the pocket (woven fabric with no stretch works best), pins, fabric scissors, iron, ironing board, tape measure, hand-sewing needle, thread (match the color to the pocket fabric), safety pins, scissors/thread snips

Sewing machine? Use a straight stitch instead of a running stitch where indicated in the following steps

Top Tip

When choosing a fabric for your patch pocket, anything goes when it comes to color or pattern. But ensure you opt for a medium- or heavyweight woven fabric with no stretch.

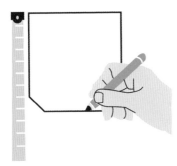

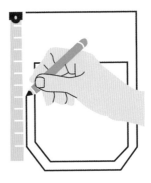

1 Design the rough shape of your pocket in the center of the paper; check that it is big enough to put your hand in easily. When you're happy with the size, use a ruler to make straight edges straight, and check any curves are smooth and even.

2 Add 1⅝in (4 cm) to the opening edge. Then add ⅜in (1 cm) to the other edges and draw these new lines. Cut along this new outer edge with paper scissors for your pocket template.

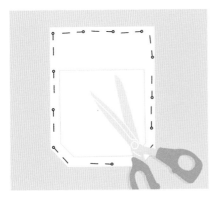

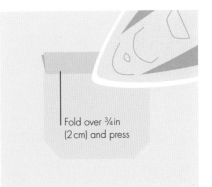

Fold over ¾in (2 cm) and press

3 Position your paper pocket template on your fabric and pin it in place. Use your fabric scissors to cut out the pocket shape from the fabric. Repeat for however many pockets you'd like to add.

4 Lay the pocket piece right-side down, turn the opening edge back ¾in (2 cm). Press this fold. Turn the edge back by another ¾in (2 cm) and press again. Thread a needle with a length of thread about 12 in (30 cm) long. Tie a knot in one end. **»**

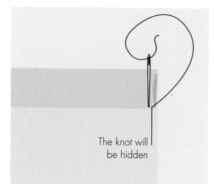

The knot will
be hidden

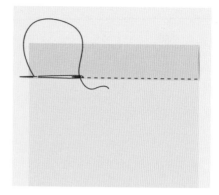

5 Still with the pocket piece right-side down, make a running stitch, close to the inner fold at the opening edge. Push the needle up through all layers. Pull the needle back down, about ³⁄₁₆in (5 mm) away from where it first emerged.

6 Pull the needle and thread down from behind, then repeat step 5 to make a row of even running stitches. Make two small stitches on top of each other over the final running stitch. Trim the excess thread. The opening edge is now finished.

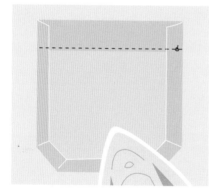

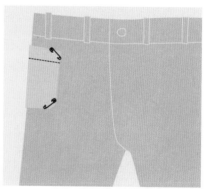

7 Fold the remaining edges of the pocket piece in by ³⁄₈in (1 cm). Press the edges. (If a pocket includes curves, fold and press carefully to avoid any harsh lines.) Flip the pocket piece over, so the right side faces up, and press to set the shape.

8 Pin the pocket to your garment with safety pins in roughly the right position. Pockets need to be accessible and keep their contents safe, but where you put them is up to you. Try on the garment to check the position and adjust as necessary.

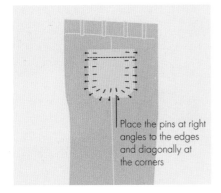

Place the pins at right angles to the edges and diagonally at the corners

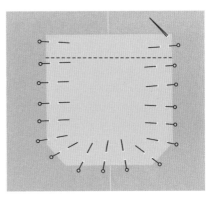

9 Lay the garment on a flat surface. Add dressmaking pins to stabilize the pocket in its final position. Place the pins about 1 in (2.5 cm) apart, perpendicular to the edges. Do not pin the opening edge. Pin through a single layer of the garment only.

10 Thread a needle with an 18 in (45 cm) length of thread (longer for a large pocket). Tie a knot in one end. Starting at the top corner, about ⅛ in (3 mm) from the edge, push the needle up from behind through the garment and the pocket.

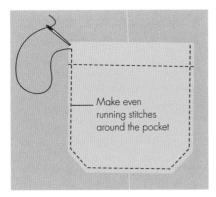

Make even running stitches around the pocket

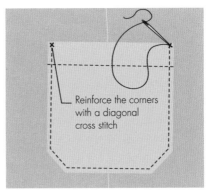

Reinforce the corners with a diagonal cross stitch

11 Pull the needle and thread out from above and push them back down, about ³⁄₁₆ in (5 mm) away. Continue around the pocket with even running stitches. At the back, make two small stitches on top of each other, through the garment only.

12 Prepare a needle and a double thickness of thread (see p.30). At both the top corners, push the needle up from behind and make a diagonal stitch. Stitch over this a few times, then repeat in the opposite direction to make an "X."

Patch pockets

CHANGE THE LOOK OF A GARMENT
BY MAKING AND ADDING FUNCTIONAL
PATCH POCKETS OR DECORATIVE PATCH
POCKETS FOR FUN.

Refitting a garment at the seams

Reducing the volume of a garment by taking it in at the seams can have a major impact on its overall look. Follow these steps to give a fresh, refined feel to your tops, dresses, jeans, skirts, T-shirts, and knitwear. Basically any unlined garment is fair game!

You will need pins, fabric-marking tool, tape measure, hand-sewing needle, color-matched thread, scissors/thread snips, fabric scissors

Sewing machine? Use a straight stitch where a running stitch is indicated in step 4

Top Tip

Resist the urge to make your garment overly fitted. You still need to move, reach, bend, and sit down comfortably in it. Remove a conservative amount of material to begin with; you can always pinch more out later.

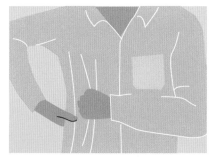

1 Try the garment on in front of a mirror. You can make skirts, trousers, dresses, and tops more form-fitting by pinching out fabric at the side seams; and you can slim down sleeves at the seam, too. Play around with pinching out fabric along the seams with your fingers and/or pins to find the look you want; it's easier to do this with the item the right way around. Remove any pins.

2 Take off the garment, turn it inside out, and put it back on. Recreate your desired look by placing pins parallel to the seam to indicate a new stitching line. Make sure you reduce the volume evenly on both sides of the garment. Carefully take the garment off with the pins still in place.

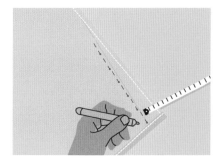

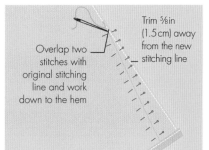

Overlap two stitches with original stitching line and work down to the hem

Trim ⅝in (1.5cm) away from the new stitching line

3 Lay the garment out on a flat surface. Use a fabric-marking tool to mark the new stitching line shown by the pins. Blend the new stitching line smoothly into the original stitching. Repeat on the other seam. Use a tape measure to check that the same amount is being taken out of both seams. Remove the pins.

4 Stabilize the stitching line by placing pins perpendicular to the seam. Prepare your needle and thread as in step 2 on p.37. Use running stitch along your marked line (refer to steps 4–6 on p.63, if necessary); repeat on the other side of the garment. Trim excess fabric ⅝in (1.5cm) away from the new stitching line.

Refitting using waist-shaping darts

Almost any hip-length or longer garment that feels a bit shapeless can be refined to feel and look more elegant. You can easily alter dresses, tunics, shirts, blouses, and tops without affecting the look from the front at all. Witchcraft? No. Waist-shaping darts? Yes.

You will need Pins, tape measure, fabric-marking tool, ruler, hand-sewing needle, color-matched thread, scissors/thread snips, iron, ironing board

Sewing machine? Use a straight stitch where a running stitch is indicated in step 10

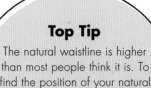

Top Tip

The natural waistline is higher than most people think it is. To find the position of your natural waist, stand facing a mirror and bend your body to the side. Place your hand where your torso creases: this is your natural waistline.

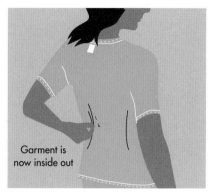

Garment is
now inside out

1 Try the garment on in front of a mirror. Play around with pinching fabric evenly on both sides of your back at your natural waist (see Top Tip); it's easier to see with the garment the right way out. Pinch different amounts, but resist over-fitting.

2 Turn the garment inside out and put it back on. Recreate the desired effect and place a pin vertically in each side at your natural waistline. Aim to pin the fabric by the same amount at each dart position. Ask a friend to help if possible/necessary.

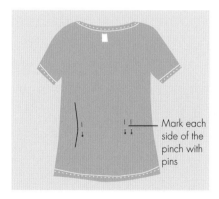

Mark each
side of the
pinch with
pins

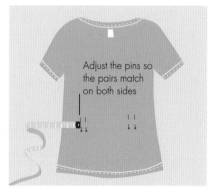

Adjust the pins so
the pairs match
on both sides

3 Carefully take off the garment and lay it on a flat surface inside out, ready to mark the darts. Place a pin vertically on either side of the fabric at the pinch. Remove the original pin so the fabric can lay flat. Repeat on the other side.

4 Measure the distance from the side seam to the nearest vertical pin on both sides. Add these measurements together and divide by two to get the average distance from the side seam to outer edge of the dart. Write this number down. **»**

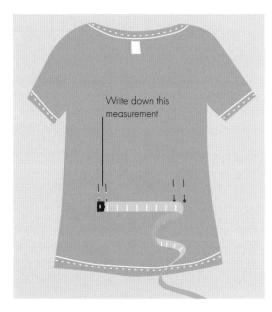

Write down this
measurement

Note: You may find it useful to practice steps 4 to 9 using your measurements to plot the darts on paper first, before marking the actual garment. It will be difficult to remove any plotting mistakes on the actual fabric.

5 Measure the distance between each pair of vertical pins. Add them together and divide by two to get an average width for each dart. Write this down. With these numbers, you can start to plot your dart onto the fabric.

Use a fabric-marking tool to make a vertical mark

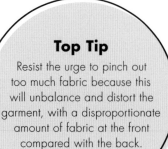

Top Tip
Resist the urge to pinch out too much fabric because this will unbalance and distort the garment, with a disproportionate amount of fabric at the front compared with the back.

6 Remove the pins. At the natural waist, measure across from the side seam and draw a vertical mark at the measurement from step 4. Make a second mark for the width of the dart, using the number from step 5. Repeat on the other side.

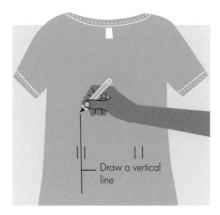

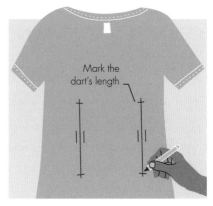

7 The width of the darts are now plotted. To plot their length, start by drawing a vertical line through the center of the dart, perpendicular to the waistline. Extend the line at least 6 in (15 cm) above and 6 in (15 cm) below the waistline.

8 If the width of your dart is 1⅜ in (3.5 cm) or more, make a small horizontal mark on the long vertical line 6 in (15 cm) above and below the waistline. If it is less than 1⅜ in (3.5 cm) wide, make the mark 4¾ in (12 cm) above and below the waistline.

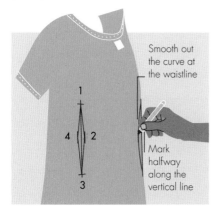

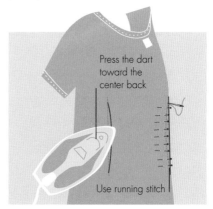

9 Draw straight lines to connect the four points to form a long diamond shape. Fold the garment along the vertical line, right-sides together. Redraw the point at the waistline so it becomes a smooth curve. Repeat on the other side.

10 Keep the fabric flat and in position by placing pins perpendicular to the dart. Follow steps 3 to 6 in Mending a tear on p.59 to make a row of running stitches following the line. Stitch both darts, then gently press them toward the center back.

Making a garment larger

"It's just a bit small" is a common reason not to wear an item. While we can't magically make an item bigger, we can insert a strip into side and sleeve seams to size-up a top or dress.

You will need   seam ripper, tape measure, fabric-marking tool, insert fabric (match to garment fabric type), fabric scissors, iron, ironing board, hand-sewing needle, thread (match color to the garment), scissors/thread snips, pins

Sewing machine?   For hemming (step 4): for woven fabrics, use a straight stitch; for knits, use a three-step or wide zigzag stitch. For attaching the insert (step 6): for woven fabrics, use a straight stitch; for knit fabrics, use a narrow zigzag, which will allow the seam to stretch a little

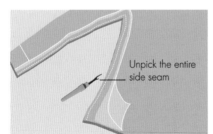

Unpick the entire side seam

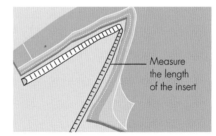

Measure the length of the insert

1 Carefully unpick the side seams and sleeve seams of the garment. If the garment is sleeveless and has an armhole facing, unpick the side seam of the facing, too, then treat the outer and facing layers as one in the following steps.

2 Measure the length of the seam from sleeve hem (or armhole) to the garment hem. Add 1⅝in (4cm) to this figure to find the length of the insert. Gauge how wide you'd like the insert to be and add double the garment's original seam allowance.

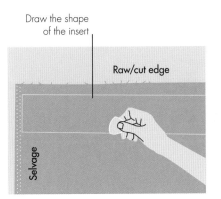

Draw the shape of the insert

Raw/cut edge

Selvage

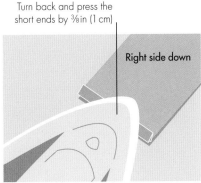

Turn back and press the short ends by ⅜ in (1 cm)

Right side down

3 Using a fabric-marking tool, mark this rectangle out on your insert fabric and cut it out. It may be necessary to make a join with running stitches if the rectangle length measurement is particularly long.

4 Turn the short ends back by ⅜ in (1 cm), press, then turn again by ⅜ in (1 cm) and press. Thread a needle with 12 in (30 cm) of thread and tie a knot in one end. Make small running stitches close to the hem at both short ends.

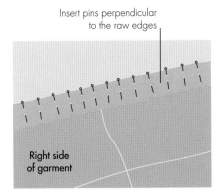

Insert pins perpendicular to the raw edges

Right side of garment

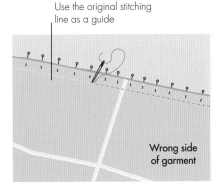

Use the original stitching line as a guide

Wrong side of garment

5 With right sides together, position the insert along one of the side seams (and sleeve seam, as necessary), aligning the raw edges. Match the insert's hems with the garment's hem and sleeve hem or underarm. Insert pins at regular intervals.

6 Thread a needle with 18 in (45 cm) of thread and tie a knot in one end. With the garment fabric wrong side up, make small, neat running stitches to attach the insert. Pin the other edge of the insert as for step 5; repeat to sew the other side.

Removing sleeves

Fitting techniques are excellent for streamlining the silhouette of a garment that used to be too big. But how do we approach a garment that is too small? If tight sleeves are the issue, a simple option is to remove them completely.

You will need **For woven garments:** seam ripper, scissors/thread snips, pins, tape measure, 39 in (1 m) bias tape, fabric scissors, hand-sewing needle, color-matched thread, iron, ironing board

For knit/jersey garments: fabric scissors, pins, tape measure, scissors/thread snips, hand-sewing needle, color-matched thread, iron, ironing board

Sewing machine? Use a straight stitch where a running stitch is indicated in steps 6, 7, and 12 (pp.107–108); use a three-step zigzag stitch in step 4 on p.109

Top Tip

The success of this technique relies on being able to envision whether the garment will look good without sleeves! New armholes will follow the line of the current sleeve seam.

For woven garments

Raw edges of woven fabric are liable to fray, so
this method employs bias tape to stabilize and
conceal the raw edge. The binding is positioned on the
inside of the garment, with only a row of small, neat
stitches visible from the outside.

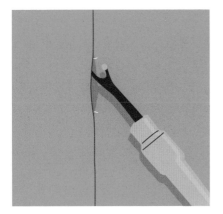

1 Using a seam ripper, carefully unpick
the stitching that attaches the sleeves.
If the garment is lined, unpick the stitching
that attaches the sleeve lining as well.
Remove any loose threads or broken
stitches from around the armholes.

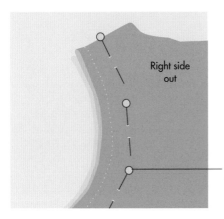

Right side
out

Place the pins parallel to
the new raw edge

2 If the garment is lined, pin the outer
and lining together around the armholes
with pins placed parallel to the new raw
edge, about ⅝ in (1.5 cm) away from the
original stitching line. Then, you'll be able
to treat both layers as one in the following
steps. **»**

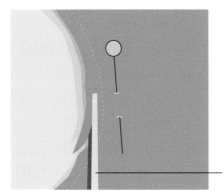

3 The former stitching line around the armhole will still be visible thanks to the perforations in the fabric. Trim the seam allowance around the armholes so only ¼in (7 mm) remains between the raw edge and the former stitching line.

Use scissors to remove some fabric around the armhole

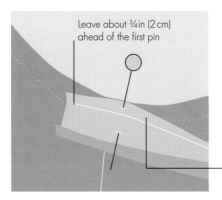

Leave about ¾in (2 cm) ahead of the first pin

4 Holding the bias tape face down, open up the top fold and align the outer edge with the raw edge at the bottom of the armhole. Leave the first ¾in (2 cm) of the bias tape loose, extending beyond the side seam. Place a pin through all layers, perpendicular to the edges.

Place right sides together

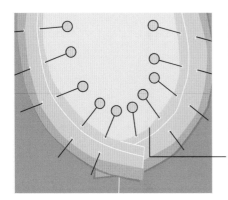

5 Continue to align the outer edge of the bias tape with the raw edge of the armhole all the way around, keeping the bias tape flat and avoiding tucks or pleats. Pin as you go. When the bias tape reaches the starting point, cut off the remainder leaving ¾in (2 cm) loose at the end, extending beyond the side seam.

Align the bias tape's outer edge with the raw edge on the garment

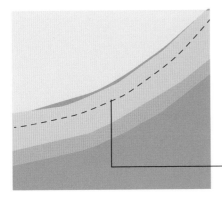

6 Thread a needle with a length of sewing thread no longer than 18 in (45 cm). Tie a knot at one end of the single strand of thread. Using small, neat, running stitches, stitch the bias tape to the garment all around the armhole. Use the crease in the bias tape as your guide. Remove the pins.

Follow the crease in the bias tape

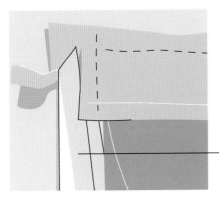

7 Open up the other fold of the bias tape and carefully press it flat. Position the loose ends of bias tape right-sides facing, and using small, neat running stitches, stitch them together across their width. Trim the excess bias tape ¼ in (7 mm) away from the line of stitching.

Trim the excess bias tape after stitching

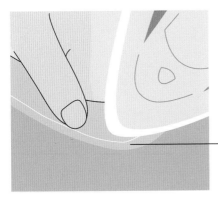

8 Turn the garment inside out. Flip the bias tape to the inside. If your garment fabric can withstand heat, carefully press the edge of the armhole curve to set the crease. A little steam will help the bias tape mold around the curve. **»**

Press the bias tape so it follows the curve of the armhole

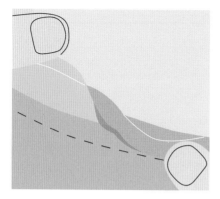

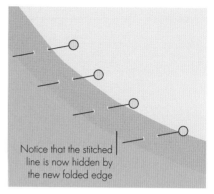

Notice that the stitched line is now hidden by the new folded edge

9 Open the bias tape up so the running stitches are visible. Bring the outer raw edge of the bias tape to meet the stitching. Then, fold the bias tape back down into position with the right side facing up, and carefully press to set the new fold.

10 Continuing to work from the wrong side of the garment, place pins diagonally through all layers to keep the bias tape in place. Position the pins at regular intervals around the armhole.

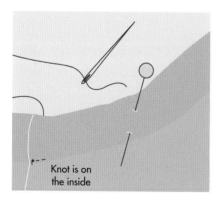

Knot is on the inside

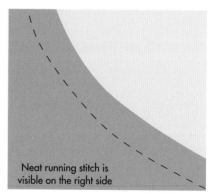

Neat running stitch is visible on the right side

11 Rethread the needle following step 6 (p.107). Starting at the bottom of the armhole, push the needle down through all layers close to the bias tape's folded edge and pull through from below, so that the knot is on the inside of the garment.

12 Make small, neat running stitches close to the folded lower edge of the bias tape to keep it permanently in position. Remove the pins, give the binding a final press, and turn the garment right side out.

For knit/jersey garments

If you want to remove sleeves from a T-shirt or jersey garment, use this simpler method. Because the raw edges of knit fabrics rarely fray, there's no need for bias tape.

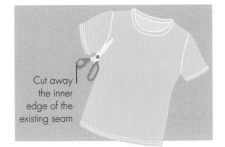

Cut away the inner edge of the existing seam

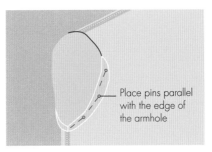

Place pins parallel with the edge of the armhole

1 Knit garments are more difficult to unpick than woven garments due to the risk of stretching the fabric. Carefully cut the sleeves off instead, cutting away the seam allowances as well as the sleeves.

2 Handle the raw edges with care until the armhole has been stitched. Turn the garment inside out. Carefully fold the raw edge back ⅜ in (1 cm) to the inside. Pin in place around the edge of the armhole.

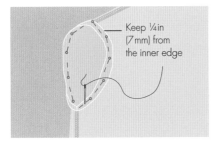

Keep ¼ in (7 mm) from the inner edge

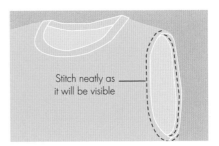

Stitch neatly as it will be visible

3 Thread a needle with no more than 18 in (45 cm) of thread and tie a knot at one end. Starting at the bottom of the armhole, push the needle down through both layers about ¼ in (7 mm) from the inner folded edge of the armhole.

4 Making small, neat running stitches, continue to stitch around the armhole. Keep the stitching quite loose (to allow for some stretch when dressing and undressing). Remove the pins as you go. Press the armholes and turn the item right side out.

Adding elastic to hems and cuffs

Another way to modify a garment's silhouette is to transform the volume of full sleeves and wide trouser legs with some clever elastic.

You will need

Super-speedy method: seam ripper, tape measure, 39 in (1 m) elastic, scissors/thread snips, 2 large safety pins, hand-sewing needle, color-matched thread

Creating a channel: pins, tape measure, fabric-marking tool, 39 in (1 m) elastic, fabric scissors, iron, ironing board, scissors/thread snips, hand-sewing needle, color-matched thread, 2 large safety pins

Sewing machine? Use a straight stitch where a running stitch is indicated in step 5 on p.113

Top Tip
This technique is best applied to garments made from light- and medium-weight fabrics, and is suitable for both wovens and knits.

Super-speedy method

If you want to keep the length, and the measurement between the very bottom edge of the cuff and the hem stitching is at least ½in (1cm) or so, then opt for this swift method.

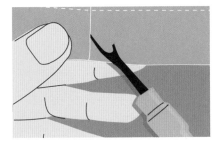

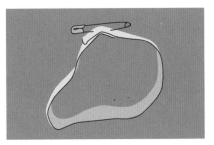

1 With the garment inside out, find the section of hem where the sleeve or inside leg seam are visible. Carefully unpick the seam stitching between the bottom folded edge and the hem stitching.

2 Measure the distance between the bottom folded edge and the hem stitching. Select elastic that is slightly narrower than this, cut off a generous piece, overlap the ends, and secure with a safety pin.

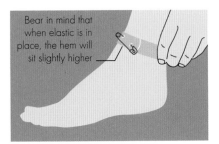

Bear in mind that when elastic is in place, the hem will sit slightly higher

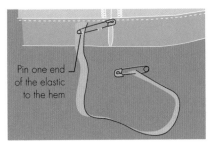

Pin one end of the elastic to the hem

3 Try the elastic at the position where the garment hem will sit. Adjust the loop until it feels snug but not uncomfortable. Allowing ¾in (2cm) for the ends to overlap, cut two pieces of elastic the correct length.

4 Affix a safety pin to one end of the elastic and attach to the inner edge of the hem. Securing the elastic will prevent it from getting lost inside. Put the second safety pin through the other end. **»**

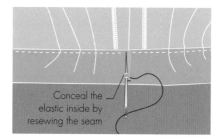

Secure the overlap with a safety pin

Conceal the elastic inside by resewing the seam

5 Insert the free safety-pinned end into the hole in the seam. Feed it through the channel until it emerges, checking that it hasn't twisted. Pull the ends away from the item and remove both safety pins. Overlap the ends by ¾in (2 cm) and repin.

6 Feed the elastic back into the channel. Try the garment on to check that the elastic feels right. Then, secure by stitching up and down through both layers of elastic at the overlap. Close up the hole at the hem using a ladder stitch (see pp.61–62).

Creating a channel

If you want to shorten the length as well as elasticizing the hem, you'll need a new channel. If the original hems are too narrow, follow this method but omit steps 1 and 3.

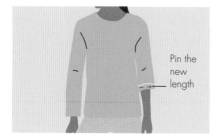

Pin the new length

Wide elastic looks more sporty

Narrow elastic looks more delicate

1 Try on the item in front of a mirror. Turn up the hem and pin. Assess the new length; adjust if needed. The elastic will lift the hem slightly, so add a little extra to compensate.

2 Select an appropriate width of elastic. If you wish to retain as much length as possible, pick a narrow elastic; avoid elastic that is narrower than ⅜in (1 cm).

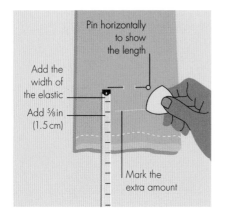

Pin horizontally
to show
the length

Add the
width of
the elastic

Add ⅝in
(1.5 cm)

Mark the
extra amount

Pin horizontally
to secure the
channel

Fold back to create
the channel and
hide raw edges

3 Follow step 2 of Shortening a hem on pp.82–83. Measure the width of the elastic, add ⅝in (1.5 cm), and mark this extra amount. Follow step 4 on p.83 to remove the excess fabric from the hems.

4 With the garment inside out, fold back the bottom edge by ⅜in (1 cm) and press. Then, fold back the width of the elastic plus ³⁄₁₆in (5 mm) and press again. Pin this channel about ¼in (7 mm) from its top edge.

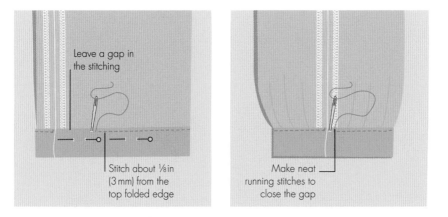

Leave a gap in
the stitching

Stitch about ⅛in
(3 mm) from the
top folded edge

Make neat
running stitches to
close the gap

5 Starting at the inner seam, make a line of small, neat running stitches. Leave a 1³⁄₁₆in (3 cm) gap in the stitching to thread the elastic through. Follow steps 4 and 5 on p.111–112 to insert the elastic.

6 Feed the elastic back into the channel. Try the garment on to check that the elastic feels right. Then, secure by stitching up and down through both layers of elastic at the overlap. Close the gap with running stitch.

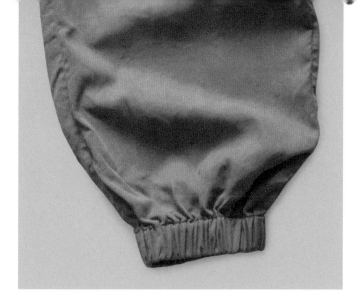

Elasticized sleeves and trouser hems

MAKE A BOLD STATEMENT—MODIFY THE SILHOUETTE OF WIDE SLEEVES AND PANT LEGS WITH SOME ELASTIC.

Love Your Clothes

Introduction

You're fixing damaged garments. You're transforming abandoned garments into something wearable for you or a friend. Everything in your wardrobe is looking great and working well. Now, it's time to talk about the long term.

Well done, you! You've been taking the time to learn an array of new skills to fix the flaws in your clothes. And you've expanded upon that further, brandishing new techniques to customize and adapt existing clothing to your specifications. These are fun, heady, creative times, aren't they? Hopefully you're still in the throes of rekindled passion for the garments that you've already worked on. But now it's time to talk about caring for your clothes in the long term.

Future-proofing your wardrobe

In this chapter we'll cover storage methods for both regularly used and off-season clothing (including how to prevent moth damage), laundry and ironing tips, tactics for treating or hiding stains, and how to dive into the world of dyeing.

Granted, garment care may not be as exciting as learning and flexing new and interesting skills. But the "slow-fashion" ethos is as much about soaking a tea-stained T-shirt in cold water, as it is about sashiko-style stitching. All that awesome mending and innovative reworking will be undermined

if you don't take good care of those newly improved garments. You owe it to yourself and to the clothes to go the extra mile and learn how best to look after them. Only then can they perform their functions successfully, while looking great for as long as possible.

The all-important storage

First up, we will brush up on how best to keep your clothing when it is not being worn. Whether you wear the garment all the time or it is in its off-season, all garments

All that awesome mending and innovative reworking will be undermined if you don't take good care of those newly improved garments.

deserve to be put away and stored correctly. So, what approaches will help them keep their structure well? Which items definitely need to be hung up and which should be folded?

How can you maximize storage space so that all your options are accessible and nothing becomes lost, forgotten, or overlooked. And is there anything to be done to prevent the biggest causes of wardrobe wreckage—moths and mold or mildew? We'll give you all the answers.

The biggest takeaway to be had is to wash your garments as infrequently as you can get away with.

Laundry aficionado

Presumably you've already been doing your own laundry (and possibly other people's) for some time. So, it might seem a bit weird to be boning up on laundry techniques at this stage as, by now, it's most likely something that you just do. Yet, it's the actions that are performed day in and day out that keep your garments healthy and functioning well or lead them to become prematurely faded and misshapen.

When we talk of garment care, what does that really mean? Keeping it fresh and clean by laundering it regularly? No! The biggest takeaway to be had is to wash your clothes as infrequently as you can get away with. Nothing weakens and fades clothing quicker than washing after every wear (undies, base wear, and socks are exempt).

Discovering which approaches to washing and drying are kinder to the planet greatly affects how much or little a garment impacts the environment over its lifetime.

Garment refreshers

At risk of sounding like a detergent advertisement, coffee spills, pasta sauce splashes, sweat marks, and baby poop (even on pale garments) needn't make you roll your eyes and announce, "Well, that's ruined". If you discover the right approaches and deal with it quickly, you should be able to get rid of that stain completely.

Refreshing a garment's color or changing it up entirely is also a way to enliven a well-worn pair of jeans or perk up an old T-shirt. Learning the basics of which fabrics take dye best and types of dye will enable you to branch out into a world of color. And if all efforts at stain removal fail, then disguise marks with a cute embroidery detail with a little needle and thread action.

There is a real satisfaction from caring properly for garments that you have invested in. While efforts may not always be visible, it doesn't mean they can't be appreciated.

Smart storage options

Use these tips for storing your clothes, whether in regular rotation or packed away for their off-season. Your rewards are clothes that stay in the best possible shape longer and remain undamaged by moths, mold, or mildew.

Even with garments that you wear often, there are certain storage methods and practices that are good to stick to. These will give your clothes their best shot at looking good for as long as possible.

The general rule is: structured garments and those that require ironing should be hung up; everything else either can or definitely should be put away flat (folded or rolled). Jeans, cords, and robust trousers can be hung or folded, depending on space. Knitwear and knit fabric garments, including T-shirts, knit dresses, and sweatshirts, should always be folded or rolled so their weight doesn't distort their shape.

Hang it up

Keep structured coats and jackets hung up on wide, sturdy hangers that properly extend into the shoulders. Coats and jackets, as well as other button-up garments such as shirts, blouses, and shirt-dresses, are all best kept with their top button done up, plus at least every other one, to help

retain their structure. Never use wire coat hangers because they can rub and damage the fabric over time.

Don't cut off the hanging loops

If your hanging garments include hanging loops, use them. The loops help distribute the pressure put on the garment when it's hung up. They also keep slippery garments from sliding off their hangers and ending up in a pile at the bottom of the closet.

Customize clip hangers

The ideal skirt hangers include padding where the hanger grips the garment to prevent indentations. If yours do not have these, insert rectangles of fabric between the clips to sandwich the garment in the middle to provide some DIY cushioning.

Keep out of the sun

Some people like clothing racks for an at-a-glance shot of what outfits are available; however, sunlight can permanently discolor

ADD PADDING TO CLIP HANGERS

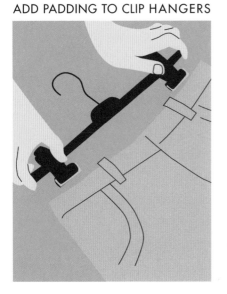

USE THE HANGING LOOPS

HANG UP STRUCTURED CLOTHES

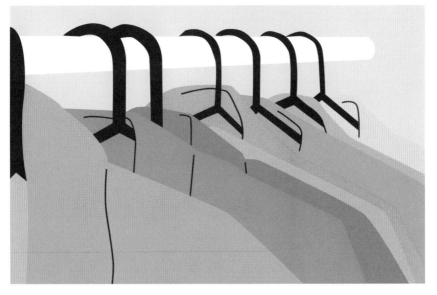

STORE AWAY FROM THE SUN

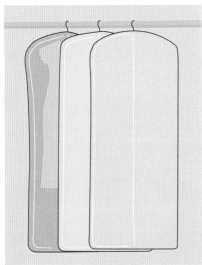

MINIATURIZE STORAGE

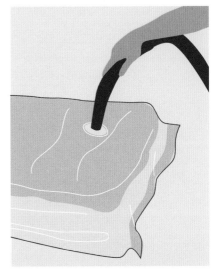

AIR YOUR CLOSET

DEHUMIDIFY IF NEEDED

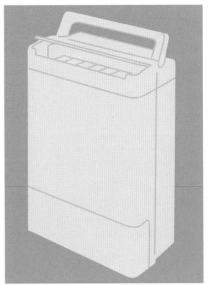

and weaken fabric, so clothes fare best inside a closet. Consider buying fabric hanging storage bags for off-season garments that need to be hung but don't fit inside a closed closet.

Fold, roll, and repeat

For garments that are stored flat in drawers or boxes, consider either rolling and storing on their sides, or folding in a way that they can be filed in rows. When you open the box or drawer, you can see the entire contents at a glance, plus it'll be easier to remove items without disturbing the contents.

Air your closet regularly

Two other causes of clothing damage are moths and mold or mildew. Like most things in life, prevention is better than cure, so keep your closet well ventilated. Moths hate light and movement, so air your closet and drawers every couple of months and move clothes around. It is their larvae, rather than the moths themselves, that cause clothing damage, so put them off wanting to make your closet their home. Vacuum your closet's corners and crevices often to nip any potential infestations in the bud.

Target the pesky moths

Moth larvae love nothing more than feasting on keratins—these are found in animal-based fibers (wool, mohair, cashmere, silk, leather, felt, and feathers). Regularly inspect these items for the first signs of holes. Wash or dry clean any clothes that do show signs of moth holes immediately. Dry cleaning is the best way to kill moth larvae. The effectiveness of mothballs and cedar repellents is debatable.

Rotate your wardrobe

The best tactic to keep air circulating around your closet is to steer clear of overfilling it. That might mean packing away out-of-season and rarely used garments. Before doing this, make sure those garments are freshly washed or dry cleaned and are bone dry. Pests are attracted to the oil from our skin and food residues.

Ban condensation

Mold and mildew are caused by condensation and damp, and there are a number of moves you can make to stop them from appearing on your clothes. Hang wet clothes out to dry as soon as possible. And check that laundry is fully dry before putting it away. If your home suffers from condensation problems, it's probably a good idea to invest in a dehumidifier product specifically for closets.

Find a permanent storage that works

There are various types of containers available for packing away clothing. All appear to have their pros and cons, but arguably, air-tight plastic storage bins or vacuum or compression storage bags should provide the best protection from both pests and damp.

Laundry and ironing tips

How, and how often, you wash your clothes greatly affects the lifespan of garments. And laundering accounts for a huge proportion of a garment's carbon footprint. Discover how to treat both your clothing and the planet with care.

However long you've been doing the washing, learn how new laundry habits can benefit your newly revamped wardrobe.

Wash clothes less

Before automatically throwing a garment into the laundry basket, ask yourself if it really needs washing. If a garment has had no contact with sweat and isn't stained, you can wear it multiple times before you need to wash it. Repeated laundering breaks down the fibers and fades colors, making garments look old and worn more quickly. And clothes made from synthetic fibers release microplastics with each wash, which enter waterways and the food chain.

Naturally neutralize smells

Don't rush to wash clothing that looks fine, but smells a little musty or has lingering odors from cooking and so on. Neutralize the smell by hanging it up for a couple of hours by an open window or in an outside space. Another option is the "hang it while you shower" approach—the steam encourages the fibers to release any odor particles and any wrinkles, too.

Out, damned spot!

If an otherwise clean-looking garment is sporting a small mark, avoid the damage a full wash will do by spot-cleaning instead. A more extensive guide to the removal and pretreatment of all kinds of stains is on pp.128–129. But the best way to deal with a small stain is to rub the marked area with the corner of a clean, damp cloth and some hand soap. Rub again with a soap-free corner of the damp cloth and leave to dry.

Wash like with like

Always separate your light-, bright-, and dark-colored fabrics and wash like-with-like to avoid dye run-off and prematurely tired-looking clothes. Get to know which garments require handwashing or dry cleaning by checking the garment care labels, and wash everything else at 86°F or

WASH INFREQUENTLY

FRESHEN UP OUTDOORS

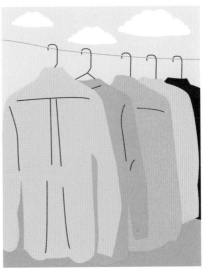

SPOT-CLEAN SMALL MARKS

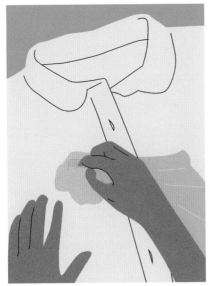

SEPARATE LIGHTS AND DARKS

HAND-WASH DELICATE ITEMS

STEAM OUT WRINKLES

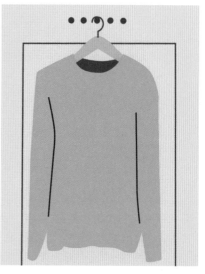

LINE DRY IF POSSIBLE

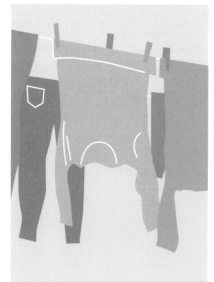

IRON INSIDE OUT

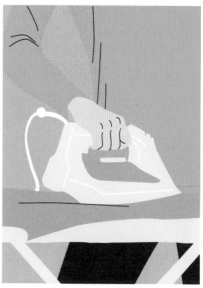

104°F max. Fasten any zippers or buttons to prevent damage, and wash all garments inside out to reduce pilling caused by the friction of garments rubbing together.

Hands down: the best method

Tailored garments such as coats and jackets will need professional dry cleaning to retain their shape. However, unstructured and soft garments that are labeled "dry clean only" can be hand-washed instead of professional dry cleaned. Always clean the sink you will be using to avoid traces of grease being transferred onto clothes. Make sure the water temperature is cold or tepid, and use a laundry detergent specifically designed for handwashing. After handwashing, you can hang lightweight garments to drip dry. Lie heavier-weight items such as knitwear flat on a towel to dry, as hanging may distort the shape of the garment.

Line drying is best

Tumble drying takes a massive toll on your clothes; the additional friction and intense heat creates pilling, weakens and breaks down fibers, and can cause shrinking and fading. It also uses an enormous amount of energy—for a typical load that was washed at 104°F then dried in a tumble dryer, 75 percent of the carbon footprint is attributed to the drying. Hanging clothes outside on a line or drying rack, whenever possible, will do wonders for the longevity of your clothing, and significantly lessen their environmental impact. When the weather is poor or if you

have no outside space, consider hanging laundry on a clothes horse or drying rack in a well-ventilated room where it won't get in your way. A bathroom that sees little use during the day with a window open is ideal.

The iron-free approach

Ironing is another laundry process that can damage clothing and uses energy that might be avoided entirely. Ward off the formation of wrinkles by removing your clean clothes from the machine as soon as the wash cycle ends. Give each garment a good shake and peg or hang it out as flat as possible. Steam helps creases drop out of clothing (as well as odors, see also p.124), so it's worth hanging an item up in the bathroom while you take a shower if there's time—it may avoid having to get the ironing board out altogether.

Ironing out the wrinkles

When ironing is necessary, always check the garment care label to find the recommended temperature setting before you start. Temperature settings on individual irons can fluctuate, so test the chosen setting out on a less-visible section of the garment before starting with the rest of the task. Where possible, iron clothing inside out. The heat and pressure from ironing can create permanent shiny areas that make a garment look older and more worn than it is. When and where it is necessary to iron on the right side of the garment, use a pressing cloth (see p.49) to reduce potential damage.

Stains and how to remove them

Nothing spoils the look of a garment quite like an ugly stain. We'll look at some approaches for pretreatment and dealing more generally with some common stain-makers to avoid them becoming permanent.

No matter what the substance is that is threatening to stain your clothing, first try to get as much off as you can. Use a clean, dry cloth to blot up liquid spills. With thick, gloppy things—sauces, for instance—scrape off as much as possible with a spoon or knife. Start from the edge of the blob and scrape inward to avoid spreading it further.

As we've seen (see p.127), to improve clothing longevity and to reduce our carbon footprint, tumble drying our clothes should ideally be a last resort. Never use them to dry clothing that has been stained, because it will set the stain permanently. A wet garment may fool you into thinking it's stain-free, but you cannot really tell until it is dry, so don't risk the tumble dryer. Better still, if possible, allow the garment to dry outside in direct sun—sunlight has amazing stain-removal powers.

Top Tip
If all attempts to remove an unsightly stain have failed and it's too large to hide, then consider dyeing the garment (see p.130).

A GUIDE TO STAIN REMOVAL

Stains	How best to treat
Tea and coffee	There's a reason why coffee and tea can be used to dye cloth: they leave a permanent stain. Sprinkle salt or baking soda to cover a coffee stain as soon as possible. Leave it for a while, then rinse off. For tea stains, run under cold water immediately, gently rubbing the fabric to try to lift the stain. If the stain remains, soak light-colored fabrics in a chlorine bleach solution; for dark and bright colors, try mixing equal parts of white vinegar and salt and gently rubbing onto the stain. Rinse with cold water and wash as usual.
Blood and baby poop	The worst thing for protein-based stains, like blood and baby poop, is heat—no 140°F wash is going to shift this mark. Rinse the area with cold water while the stain is fresh. If possible, put it straight into the machine on a cold cycle; if not, soak the item in cold water until you can pop it in that cold wash, but avoid soaking for longer than 10–12 hours, as the stain will be more likely to set. Absolutely do not tumble dry or iron until you're sure the stain is gone.
Makeup and greasy foods	For oil-based stains—makeup, greasy food, and sauces—there are a couple of avenues of attack, depending on what you have on hand. First, slip some cardboard or a magazine underneath the stain to protect the fabric below. Apply a spot of dish-washing liquid directly to the stained area. With a damp, clean cloth, rub the stain in a circular motion, working from the outside in to avoid it spreading. Rinse the dish-washing liquid out and wash as usual. Another approach is to use a powder to lift the oil out of the fibers. You can apply cornstarch, baking powder, or talcum powder to draw out the grease. Leave cornstarch on for 10 minutes, baking powder for 30 minutes, and talcum powder overnight if necessary. Then, dust off the remaining powder. If the stain remains, blot with a damp, clean cloth before putting in the wash.
Sweat	Yellow sweat stains look unappealing, but luckily there are two substances we can turn to for help. The first is baking soda. Mix it with water to make a paste, then apply it to the fabric. If the fabric isn't delicate, scrub the paste into the stain. Leave for an hour then rinse off. The second solution is to soak the area in undiluted white vinegar for up to an hour. With an old toothbrush, very gently rub the area—sweat stains need agitation for successful removal. Then, pop in the washing machine on the hottest temperature the fabric can tolerate (be sure to check the care label).

Fabric dye transformations

Sadly, dyeing fabric is often overlooked for disguising stains and refreshing tired-looking items. Here are some pointers on extending the life of a garment with dye.

How will you embrace the world of dye and revamp your wardrobe? Choose from commercial dyes and plant-based ones.

Hand or machine dye?

You can find store-bought dyes in fabric and hardware stores, as well as online. You can choose between hand dyes or machine dyes. Hand dyeing requires you to gather together the dye pack, table salt, rubber gloves, a bucket, and a stick for stirring. Machine dye goes directly into your washing machine and is easier and potentially less messy. For bolder effects, you can use more than one dye at a time.

Natural vs synthetic fibers

Natural fibers (such as cotton, linen, wool, and silk) and regenerated fibers (rayon/viscose, modal, bamboo, Tencel/lyocell) take fabric dyes well; make sure the garment can withstand a 104°F wash if you plan to use machine dye. Dyeing fabrics that are a blend of natural or regenerated fibers and synthetic fibers, such as poly-cotton, will have a paler outcome. Dyes specifically designed for synthetics are available online.

What color is it now?

Obviously, you can achieve a more intense color when using fabric dye on white and pale-colored garments. Dyeing darker garments will have a more subtle result, so for dark clothes, it might be better to stick to matching and refreshing the original color. Colorful clothing can also be dyed, but here color theory applies—for instance, using a red-colored dye on a blue-colored fabric will result in a purple shade. Dyeing patterned fabric is totally possible, but the design will remain visible afterward.

A look at natural dyes

Regular fabric dyes do contain some potentially polluting chemicals that will end up in waterways. And while re-dyeing with regular fabric dyes will have a lower environmental impact than discarding and replacing that garment with a new one, the impact of reviving your clothing will be

CHANGE THE COLOR

TRY NATURAL DYES

EXPERIMENT WITH TIE-DYE

lessened using natural dyeing processes instead. Natural dyes can be made with items found in your garden or the supermarket—onion skins, butternut squash peelings, coffee grounds, tea leaves, avocado skins, strawberries, cherries, lavender, red cabbage, beets, celery leaves, and bamboo, to name just some. The preparation of the dye is an extra step to factor in, and they only work on pale fabrics. But if you are looking for a subtle effect, then natural dyes can bring beautiful results.

Tie-dye update

A plain garment can be reinvented and uniquely transformed with a tie-dye effect. Since regular dyeing will not cover every stain, camouflaging it with a tie-dye effect may be more effective. Tie-dye needn't result in the stereotypical hippy-style garment. Approaches to tie-dyeing range from the intricate, detailed Japanese shibori to the super-simple scrunch or crumple dyeing. And when executed with natural dyes, the effects can be delicate and artfully stylish. Plus, it's so much fun.

Don't forget the accessories!

It's not just garments that can be re-dyed. If you are re-dyeing your trusty worn-in jeans back to black again, consider throwing in those faded canvas shoes, too. If you are trying to disguise a stained T-shirt with a bold shade, why not pop in a discolored cotton tote bag and even some socks?

Dyeing

REFRESH OR ENLIVEN FADED GARMENTS
AND REINVENT YOUR WARDROBE'S
COLOR PALETTE WITH READY-TO-USE
OR NATURAL FABRIC DYES.

Disguising a stain with embroidery

What to do when a small stain or burn mark refuses to shift from an otherwise perfectly good garment? If the fabric is marked but not damaged, covering it with a patch or appliqué may seem like overkill. Yet hiding the mark with some simple, discreet embroidery might just be the sweet distraction that is required.

You will need contrasting thread/s (embroidery floss, regular thread, or darning wool for knitwear), hand-sewing needle with a large eye, scissors/thread snips, fabric-marking tool

Left-handed? Work in the opposite direction to the one shown here if that feels more comfortable

Top Tip

Embroidery thread or floss is ideal here, but a similar effect can be achieved using regular thread; use darning thread on knitwear.

A simple flower motif

Learn how to prep your thread and embroider a simple flower. Chain stitching the flower petals around the stain at its center could even look as if it was the plan all along.

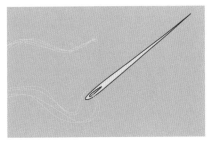

1a Cut a length of embroidery thread about 12 in (30 cm) long, separate the strands to your preferred thickness (this thread is formed from six strands), thread the needle, and tie a knot in one end.

1b For regular thread, cut about 39 in (1 m) of thread, fold it in half, wet and pinch the loop so it becomes narrow enough to thread through the needle, and then tie all the ends in a knot.

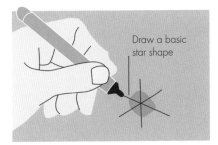

Draw a basic star shape

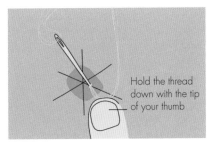

Hold the thread down with the tip of your thumb

2 With a sharp-tipped fabric-marking tool, draw a basic six-point star shape over the center of the stain. The "arms" of the star will provide a guide for the position of the six petals.

3 Push the needle up from behind, about ⅛ in (3 mm) from the center. Pull the needle and thread through from the front. Insert the needle as close as possible to where it emerged to make a loop with the thread. **»**

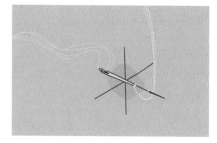

4 Angle the needle downward then push it up about ¼in (7 mm) along one of the lines. Slowly pull the needle through to form a loop. Make a tiny stitch at the outer edge of the loop to keep it in place.

5 Repeat steps 3 and 4 to form the other petals. Then, make a tiny stitch on the back of one of the petals. Pull the thread through, leaving a loop, and pass the needle through and pull tightly. Trim the thread.

Flying bug or bee motif

Use satin stitch (a "filling" stitch) here to "color in" over a stain or burn mark in the shape of a bug or bee.

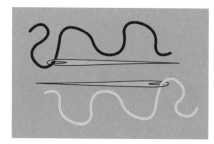

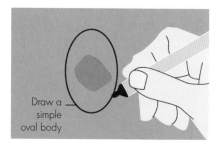

Draw a simple oval body

1 Follow step 1a or 1b on p.135 to prepare your needle and thread. Choose one color for the body of a bug or alternate between stripes of black and yellow to make a bee.

2 With a sharp-tipped fabric-marking tool, draw the body of the insect with an oval shape. Aim for a length between ⅝in (1.5 cm) and ¾in (2 cm). A crisp, clean outline will be most helpful.

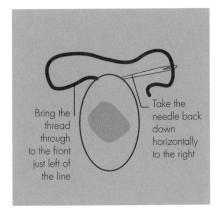

Bring the thread through to the front just left of the line

Take the needle back down horizontally to the right

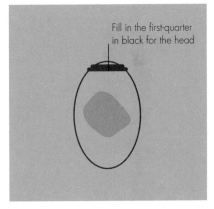

Fill in the first-quarter in black for the head

3 Push the needle up from behind at one end of the shape, slightly left of the line. Take the needle across to the line on the other side to make a straight stitch and pull it down from behind.

4 From behind, bring the needle up slightly below where it first emerged. Pull the needle and thread through from the front. Take the needle across to the line slightly below the end of the previous stitch.

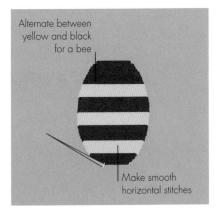

Alternate between yellow and black for a bee

Make smooth horizontal stitches

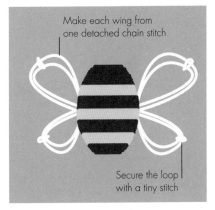

Make each wing from one detached chain stitch

Secure the loop with a tiny stitch

5 Repeat step 4, filling in the body with smooth, horizontal stitches (remember to alternate colors if you want a bee). Take care not to pull the stitches too tight or leave them loose and baggy.

6 Rethread your needle with white thread for a dark garment or black thread for a light garment. Then, follow steps 3 to 5 on pp.135–136 to make the outlines of the wings with detached chain stitch.

Using embroidery to cover stains

EMPLOY SIMPLE EMBROIDERY TO COVER
UP ANNOYING LITTLE STAINS
AND BLEMISHES THAT REFUSE TO BUDGE.

Index

Further resources

Darning, visible mending, and sashiko

Lily Fulop *Wear, Repair, Repurpose: A Maker's Guide to Mending and Upcycling Clothes*. Vermont: Countryman Press, 2020

Erin Lewis-Fitzgerald *Modern Mending: Minimize Waste and Maximize Style*. Melbourne: Affirm Press, 2020

Nina Montenegro and Sonya Montenegro *Mending Life: A Handbook for Repairing Clothes And Hearts*. Seattle: Sasquatch Books, 2020

Kerstin Neumüller *Mend & Patch: A Handbook to Repairing Clothes and Textiles*. London: Pavilion Books, 2019

Katrina Rodabaugh *Mending Matters: Stitch, Patch, and Repair Your Favorite Denim & More*. New York: Abrams, 2018

Instagram accounts to follow:
@erinlewisfitzgerald
@katrinarodabaugh
@reclaimmending
@thefarwoods
@tomofholland
@visible_creative_mending
@visiblemend

The fashion industry

Lauren Bravo *How To Break Up With Fast Fashion: A Guilt-Free Guide to Changing the Way You Shop – For Good*. London: Headline Home, 2020

Elizabeth L. Cline *Overdressed: The Shockingly High Cost of Cheap Fashion*. New York: Portfolio Books, 2013

Elizabeth L. Cline *The Conscious Closet: The Revolutionary Guide to Looking Good While Doing Good*. New York: Plume, 2019

Greta Eagan *Wear No Evil: How to Change the World with your Wardrobe*. Philadelphia: Running Press, 2014

Lucy Siegle *To Die For: Is Fashion Wearing Out the World?* London: Fourth Estate, 2011

Wardrobe Crisis podcast

www.fashionrevolution.org charity and movement working towards changing the culture and industry of fashion

www.loveyourclothes.org.uk campaign from circular-economy charity WRAP to reduce the impact of clothes on the environment

www.traid.org.uk charity working to stop clothes being thrown away

labourbehindthelabel.org charity working for garment workers' rights worldwide

Instagram accounts to follow:
@ajabarber
@fash_rev
@theseagull
@ecoage
@sophiebenson
@laurenbravo
@mrspress

Clothing care, textiles, and dyeing

Rebecca Burgess and Courtney White *Fibershed: Growing a Movement of Farmers, Fashion Activists, and Makers for a New Textile Economy*. Vermont: Chelsea Green Publishing, 2019

Rebecca Desnos *Botanical Color At Your Fingertips*. 2016

www.mamaslaundrytalk.com garment care

rebeccadesnos.com/blogs/journal natural fabric dyeing

www.tiedyeyoursummer.com techniques tie-dye techniques

Sustainable sewing and upcycling

Love to Sew podcast

refashionista.net refashioning and upcycling thrift store finds

makery.co.uk host of The Refashioners— inspiring clothing refashions and community project

timetosew.uk blog about sustainable sewing and fashion

Instagram accounts to follow:
@offset_warehouse
@sustainable.maria
@go_recreate
@sweetfindupcycled

Additional sources
[checked September 2020]

6–7 Introduction
www.greenpeace.org/international/press-release/7566/black-friday-greenpeace-calls-timeout-for-fast-fashion

https://qz.com/1212305/americans-have-stopped-trying-to-stuff-more-clothes-into-their-closets/

https://www.huffingtonpost.co.uk/entry/unworn-clothing-survey_n_5048486?guce_referrer=aHR0cHM6Ly93d3cuZ29vZ2xlLmNvbS8&guce_referrer_sig=AQAAAFLOO9bT8TXUqz2i3R6deVNT_IzgH8HLnVxN5zAG1TH_-12qOus4dt45yJUPW36CNeG8Fxb4Xm28yuUQwP-QIF5KEUKFzYyFuGwQDYUSeCV-nDosYGwSK0b1-a_IyPt1VZZYo4ttPP294Y-6Fp9yTlNLMJjrXyjey_MZtbU6zlCe&guc counter=2

www.dailymail.co.uk/femail/article-3117645/Women-ditch-clothes-ve-worn-just-seven-times-Items-left-shelf-buyer-feels-ve-weight-ve-bought-whim.html

8–11 The lowdown on "fast fashion"
www.fashionrevolution.org/usa-blog/how-much-garment-workers-really-make

news.un.org/en/story/2019/03/1035161

Dr Tara Shine *How to Save Your Planet One Object at a Time*. London: Simon & Schuster, 2020

www.fashionrevolution.org/wp-content/uploads/2017/02/What-My-Jeans-Say-About-the-Garment-Industry.pdf

www.facebook.com/unitednations/posts/10000-litres-of-water-are-needed-to-make-a-single-pair-of-jeansby-shopping-secon/10157679840810820

www.theguardian.com/sustainable-business/2015/mar/20/cost-cotton-water-challenged-india-world-water-day

www.wrap.org.uk/content/textiles-overview

http://www.weardonaterecycle.org/

Acknowledgments

Author's acknowledgments

Enormous thanks to my husband, Pat, for his love and constant belief in my abilities. You always value them highly, even when I wobble and lose focus. And thank you for helping me to find ways to write this book during lockdown, stuck in a flat with other jobs, and two small children to look after and home-school.

Massive thanks to my children, Dolores and Frankie. I hope that when the world is passed on to you and your generation, that it will be in better condition than it currently is. You push me every day to try to find ways to improve it: you are my inspiration. Just please be gentle with my sewing machine!

Thanks to Vic for supporting me through everything, all the time.

I'd like to thank my parents for raising me in a household that valued making and creating, not simply consuming. And thanks in particular to my mum for facilitating my interest in sewing, sharing her skills and knowledge, and showing me that there isn't a garment out there that can't be altered!

Thank you to the sewing community, for being the nicest, most generous, most supportive group of people there is, both IRL and on the internet!

And huge thanks to Nikki and Dawn from DK for guiding me so well through the process of writing this book. You helped make it a wonderful experience.

Publisher's acknowledgments

Dorling Kindersley would like to thank: Katie Hardwicke for proofreading, Hilary Bell for indexing, and Kate Sekules for permission to use her photographs.

Picture credits

The publisher would like to thank the following for their kind permission to reproduce their photographs:

(Key: a-above; b-below/bottom; c-centre; f-far; l-left; r-right; t-top)

34 Zoe Edwards: (t, b). 35 Zoe Edwards: (t, b). 44 Alamy Stock Photo: Carolyn Jenkins (b). Zoe Edwards: (t). 45 Dreamstime.com: Chotika (t). Zoe Edwards: (b). 54 Kate Sekules/visiblemending.com: (t, b). 55 Kate Sekules/visiblemending.com: (t, b). 76 Zoe Edwards: (t, b). 77 Zoe Edwards: (t, b). 88 Zoe Edwards: (t, b). 89 Zoe Edwards: (t, b). 94 Zoe Edwards: (t, b). 95 Zoe Edwards: (t, b). 114 Zoe Edwards: (t, b). 115 Zoe Edwards: (b). 132 Alamy Stock Photo: Helen Cowles (b). Dreamstime.com: Joloei (t). 133 Alamy Stock Photo: Emilia Kun (b); Polly Thomas (t). 138 Kate Sekules/visiblemending.com: (t, b). 139 Kate Sekules/visiblemending.com: (t, b).

All other images © Dorling Kindersley
For further information see: www.dkimages.com

About the author

Zoe Edwards is a sewing and dressmaking teacher who has been blogging about her sewing journey for over a decade. Her passions for sewing, reusing materials, and debunking fast fashion form part of her attempts to live a more sustainable and authentic life. She also aims to inspire and assist others in making their own clothing, with the firm belief that enjoying sewing needn't break the bank. She's the creator of the popular annual challenge Me-Made-May, which asks those who make their own clothing to wear it more often, or in different ways, during the month of May. The aim is to encourage people to bring the DIY and handmade ethos more firmly into their everyday lives, and to develop a better relationship with their handcrafted wardrobe. Zoe blogs at sozowhatdoyouknow.blogspot.com and is on Instagram as @sozoblog.

Senior Editors Nikki Sims, Dawn Titmus
US Editor Megan Douglass
Art Editors Amy Child, Jessica Tapolcai
Senior Production Editor Tony Phipps
Senior Production Controller Stephanie McConnell
Jacket Designer Amy Cox
Jacket Coordinator Lucy Philpott
Illustrator Steven Marsden
Managing Editor Ruth O'Rourke
Managing Art Editor Christine Keilty
Art Director Maxine Pedliham
Publishing Director Katie Cowan

First American Edition, 2021
Published in the United States by DK Publishing
1450 Broadway, Suite 801, New York, NY 10018

A catalog record for this book
is available from the Library of Congress.
ISBN: 978-0-7440-2680-1

Printed and bound in China

For the curious
www.dk.com

MIX
Paper from
responsible sources
FSC™ C018179

This book was made with Forest Stewardship
Council ™ certified paper—one small step
in DK's commitment to a sustainable future.
For more information go to
www.dk.com/our-green-pledge